MW00790397

Q & A

Book design by Tracy Hurren and Adrian Tomine. Back cover photo by May Tomine. Page 45 image courtesy of IFC Films. Page 48 image courtesy of Topic Studios.

Drawn & Quarterly books are acquired, edited, administered, marketed, and sold by: Peggy Burns, Gabrielle Cole, Trynne Delaney, Tom Devlin, Lucia Gargiulo, Tracy Hurren, Rebecca Lloyd, Alison Naturale, Julia Pohl-Miranda, Megan Tan, Reid Urchison, Shirley Wong, Francine Yulo, and the staff at our Montreal bookstore.

In memory of Kathleen Brennan and Chris Tomine.

drawnandquarterly.com | adrian-tomine.com

ISBN 978-1-77046-730-9
First edition: October 2024 | Printed in China
10 9 8 7 6 5 4 3 2 1
Cataloguing data available from Library and Archives Canada

Published in the USA by Drawn & Quarterly, a client publisher of Farrar, Straus and Giroux; published in Canada by Drawn & Quarterly, a client publisher of Raincoast Books

Q & A
Adrian Tomine

Drawn & Quarterly

INTRODUCTION

For almost thirty years now, I've had the unbelievable privilege of not only putting artwork out into the world, but also receiving feedback—mostly in the form of cards and letters—from a very engaged, thoughtful, and opinionated audience. I've spent most of those thirty years working alone, hunched over a desk in the corner of a bedroom. And while that admittedly sounds pretty grim and isolated (especially as I type this sentence, hunched over a desk in the corner of a bedroom), it's never felt that way. In fact, I often think of my career as a decades-long conversation between myself and an amorphous, mostly anonymous group of people who are for some reason drawn to my work.

The correspondence I receive is generally a mix of generous praise and ruthless critiques, as well as many, many questions—often concerning tools, process, career advice, and an array of other surprisingly random and/or personal topics. Sometimes it's uncomfortable, and occasionally it's genuinely confounding. In any case, it still means a lot to me to know that someone is responding to something I made, and it's no exaggeration to say that this feedback has affected me and my work immensely.

From 1995 to 2015 I published what I considered the most interesting of the incoming mail in each issue of my comic book series *Optic Nerve*, but I also made an effort to respond to people directly, usually with a handwritten postcard. My responses weren't particularly eloquent, but I wanted to at least acknowledge the letter-writer's interest and effort. For many years, my Sunday afternoons were devoted exclusively to this undertaking.

But things have changed. It's been a while since I've published an issue of *Optic Nerve*, and I'm not sure when I might do so again. People are generally less inclined to write letters and postcards these days, and I've been stubbornly resistant to opening a direct line of email correspondence. Most significantly, I've gotten busier, both with work and family life. (It turns out Sunday afternoons are different when you have kids!*) In recent years, my p.o. box has become mostly a vessel for political campaign flyers, shipping supply catalogs, and books in search of a blurb. For better or worse, most of the comments and queries from readers now come to me via Instagram. And to tell the truth, I have not been able to keep up with my mandate to respond to everyone—certainly not with the level of detail and insight I once strived for.

When my publisher and I began discussing this book, I thought of it as an opportunity to get back on track. The question-and-answer format initially developed as part of a "writer in residence" job that Substack offered me in 2021, and the interactive premise felt like a natural extension of those old *Optic Nerve* letters pages. My aim was to address the most common questions I've received over the years, and to do so with a greater level of

---

*See back cover.

attention than I'm usually able to provide while quickly scrolling through the messages on my phone. But I also wanted to include some of the less common questions, and basically, to avoid the typical tone and scope of a professional, journalistic interview (of which there are plenty to be found online). So we put out a call for questions, I answered them to the best of my ability, and this book is the result.

Thanks to everyone who participated, and thanks to anyone who has sent me cards, letters, or packages over the years. Contrary to the weird, uncomfortable affect I might present at a book signing (or, really, in any kind of face-to-face interaction), this connection, in all its forms, means the world to me. When I'm honest with myself, it was the reason I started all of this in the first place.

Adrian Tomine
Brooklyn, 2024

MIGHT AS WELL CHECK MY P.O. BOX WHILE I'M OUT.
WELL, THE VOLUME HAS CERTAINLY DWINDLED IN RECENT YEARS, BUT THERE'S ALWAYS AT LEAST A LITTLE BIT OF MAIL HERE TO LIFT MY SPIRITS.
IT'S HARD TO BE TOO CYNICAL WHEN THERE ARE STILL READERS OUT THERE WHO TAKE THE TIME TO SEND ME THOUGHT-FUL, HAND-WRITTEN NOTES THROUGH THE MAIL.
FPP
tomine don't be an asshole put your shit on ipad / kindle get on fb and twitter print email address check out my tumblr

Optic Nerve #13 (2013)

Q: *How the hell do you say your last name? Sorry if that's rude—long-time fan who wants to say it correctly.*

A: Not rude at all, and no surprise that this is the first question to arrive. This is literally the most frequently asked question of my career—if not my life—and I'm happy to now give a definitive answer.

There are five common mispronunciations of my last name that I usually hear, and I've become very accustomed to all of them:

TAH-min
TOE-mine
TOE-mih-nay
toe-MAY
TOE-mee-nay

Most of them make sense to me, except for "toe-MAY," which I can only guess is the result of Marisa Tomei's long-lasting impact on certain people's consciousness. The last one might be the most common variation I hear, and I attribute that (at least in part) to a strange bit of misinformation. A few years ago, a very well-respected literary journal published a supposedly definitive guide to pronouncing various authors' names. And without consulting me, they declared that the proper pronunciation of my last name was "TOE-mee-nay." Given the source, it seemed highly credible. But it was wrong!

So what's the right way to say it? Well, the way I say it (and more on this in a bit) is:

toe-MEE-neh

Okay, now that I've told you, do you think you'd be able to remember that in a year? How about in a few minutes from now? In addition to being hard to pronounce, I've come to accept that my last name is also hard to *remember* how to pronounce. I can't tell you how many times I've been involved in some kind of public event, and right before we go on stage or on air or whatever, the host says, "Okay, tell me how to say your last name." I'll usually try to put them at ease and say, "Oh, don't worry about it. No one gets it right anyway, and I don't really mind." And invariably, the host will say, "Well, *I* want to get it right!" So I'll say my name for them, and they'll repeat it correctly— we usually go back and forth a couple times just to be sure—and then as soon as we get on stage or on air or whatever, they mispronounce it.

If I sound a little wounded, I'm honestly not, and this would probably be a good time to make an important confession: *I* don't pronounce my last name correctly. When I went to Japan for the first time, I noticed that if I introduced myself to someone, they would often ask where my dad was from. At first I thought maybe they recognized the name and were trying to make some personal connection based on geography. But it turns out that, thanks to my own mispronunciation, many of those people thought my dad was European or something, and were just trying to make sense of a very unfamiliar-sounding surname. ("Is this guy half Italian or what?") When one of these people finally saw my name printed out in Japanese, they would suddenly light up as if a great mystery had been solved and say, "Ah! Toh-mee-neh!"

You might be wondering what the big difference is. I'm obviously not an expert on this, but my understanding is that the first syllable needs to be said quicker and softer, with more of a gentle "h" sound at the end. (I tend to say the first syllable like "toe"—as in the body part—but with an annoyingly Californian intonation.) The other distinction is the syllabic emphasis. I've been told that you're supposed to say all three syllables with equal weight, which I find, as a life-long English-only speaker, almost impossible. But as far as I can tell, that's the right way to do it: toh-mee-neh.

But the truth is, I don't really care how you say my last name. At this point, I actually expect it to be mispronounced, and I never bother correcting people unless they ask. I've had my name mangled by enough well-meaning people over the years to know that a mispronunciation is not an intentional slight or insult. I truly believe that most people I meet want to say my name correctly, if they only knew (or could remember) how. And like I said, I'd be quite the hypocrite if I were to get on my high horse about all this. To be honest, I give credit to anyone who at least attempts to say my name at all.

But if you're curious, I do have a *least* favorite mispronunciation, and it's "TOE-mine." It just seems like the laziest, most Anglo-centric take, but more to the point, it was for some reason the universally preferred pronunciation among my childhood tormentors, including one particular asshole gym coach.

The Loneliness of the Long-Distance Cartoonist (2020)

Q: *Have you ever had a real job?*

A: Another common question, and one that is usually tinged with at least a hint of understandable indignation.* It may not seem like it, especially to the members of my immediate family (who have only known me in my work-from-home incarnation), but the answer is: yes. I've been a dishwasher, a prep cook, a waiter, a summer school teacher, a copy maker, and a delivery driver. In most of these positions I was a mediocre employee at best, but I was especially horrible as a prep cook and a summer school teacher.

---

* My younger daughter recently went on an early morning tirade about how she has to get dressed and go to school every day, while I get to "stay home, draw, and eat soup in front of the TV."

Q: *With so many other artists and writers out there trying to get noticed, how does one bubble to the surface of the white noise and get their completed book read by agents without self-publishing or marketing?*

A: I don't know if I'm the best person to answer this question because a) I've never had a literary agent, and b) I got my start with self-publishing. But let me give it a shot.

I began my working relationship with my North American publisher (Drawn & Quarterly) more than twenty-five years ago by simply sending them copies of my self-published comics in the mail. Back then, no cartoonist had an agent. And now it seems like they all do, so maybe it's become a necessity. I'm sorry I don't have a lot of insight on the value of agents for cartoonists, but I do know that the best comics publishers are always hungry for good, new work from diverse voices, and they are still open to the possibility of that work arriving via cold submission. If there's a publisher that you feel a kinship with, look around on their website and you'll most likely find instructions on how to get your work to them. I know there's a rumor that literary book publishers won't even open an envelope if it doesn't come from an agent, but I don't think that's the case in the world of comics.

17

But also: what's wrong with self-publishing or marketing? I'm not saying you should become some obnoxious egomaniacal self-promoter, but it's also another kind of egotism to just assume that your work is so good that it will speak for itself. I've been making comics for over thirty years, and I still accept that a certain percentage of my job will have to involve some version of promotion or marketing.*

I think that even in our current digital era, making a mini-comic is still a great way to share your work with people, especially if you're just starting out. I know that when I'm at a book signing or a convention, if someone tells me their Instagram name or hands me a card with their website address on it, I probably won't remember to follow up. But if someone hands me a 'zine or mini-comic, I'll at least flip through it and certainly take notice if something about it grabs my attention. I learned a lot from my days of self-publishing, even when that meant just taking my sketchbook to the local Kinko's and making twenty-five copies of a little hand-stapled pamphlet. Something about that process, despite how primitive and small-stakes it was, allowed me to view my work with a

---

* Of course this is all assuming that you want your work to reach a wide audience and reward you financially. If that's not the case, then you *definitely* don't need an agent!

new level of objectivity and self-criticism, and somehow pushed me to try harder and improve. It also gave me something tangible that I could mail off to my favorite cartoonists—some of whom eventually promoted my work in their own comics and generously recommended me to their publishers.

I also want to acknowledge a significant word from your question: "completed." Again, I'm certainly no expert on this, but I do wonder if the "take it or leave it" method of presenting a "completed book" is always the best path for a new artist. The things I sent in to Drawn & Quarterly as submissions were little Xeroxed pamphlets, and they were never presented as the work that I hoped they would actually publish. They were more like little samples of my very-much-still-developing style, which I think, at most, showed my publisher that I might have some promise. It was an invitation to a collaborative working relationship, and I have to assume that will generally open more doors than just saying, "Do you want to publish this graphic novel or not?"

Ultimately, I think it's the quality of the work that matters the most. I'm sure that in other forms of media, it is literally impossible to be aware of every new artist that comes along, and that many a great novel or album or poetry collection or whatever has been tragically lost in the shuffle. But comics is still a relatively small world, and the people I know in all parts of the industry share a genuine desire to discover and share and discuss exciting new work. So as daunting as it may seem, I do think that just putting your work out there in any way possible—and making that work at the highest level you're capable of right now—will yield some response.

Of course I'm aware that everything I've just written is informed by personal opinions, lucky breaks, and a publishing model that might seem thoroughly antiquated to some readers. To get back to the specifics of the original question, I think "self-publishing" and "marketing" can take many forms, and you should consider doing everything you can to make your work accessible and appealing to whatever audience you hope to reach. My hunch is that this will lead to a wider range of opportunities than just trying to get an agent interested in a completed book.

Q: *What kind of pens do you use for sketches and inking?*
And also, what kind of paper works best for you?

A: I get variations on this question fairly frequently, and before I answer, I want to make the point that there are no "right" tools. When I was a kid, I was convinced that certain mysterious, elusive art supplies were the key to drawing like my cartooning idols. I would scour interviews and "how-to" books, and obsess over the specific recommended drawing tools. And then I was greatly disappointed when, after much effort and expense, I finally procured, say, a Winsor & Newton series 7 brush or a Hunt 102 nib, and my drawings still looked like shit. (I tried to avoid this bitter truth for a long time, but the tools I was really searching for were talent and experience.) For the most part, I recommend experimenting and finding the tools that produce the best results for you, even if they're not necessarily the ones your artistic heroes recommend.

I would also like to make a brief pitch on behalf of cheap tools. There are a number of art supplies that are considered cartooning staples, and are often namechecked by some of our greatest practitioners. I understand the appeal of some of these things, but I can tell you that there was a period of my life where I became overly obsessive about my artwork, and part of that was due to the fact that the supplies I was using were so damn expensive.* This was around the time I was working on the last chapter of my book *Shortcomings*. I became pre-occupied with making each page "perfect," and my pace slowed to less than a page per week. I literally threw out in-progress pages because the 400 Series Strathmore Bristol board hadn't been cut at perfectly right angles. And then I'd freak out because I'd just wasted a $5 sheet of paper.**

When I finally finished that book, I made a decision to set aside most of my fancy art supplies and start from scratch, gravitating towards the cheapest, most readily-available materials. I drew the story "Killing and Dying" using only stuff I could buy at the local Rite Aid: printer paper, a felt-tip pen (for the lettering), and a mechanical pencil (for everything else). I drew each panel on a sep-arate sheet of printer paper, using only those two tools. And not to be overly dramatic here, but it was pretty lib-erating. If a panel wasn't going the way I wanted, I just crumpled up the paper and started over. Being freed from the anxiety of making a perfect, complete page with

---

* The other part was just low-grade OCD.

** Okay, maybe the OCD wasn't that low-grade.

the "right" tools allowed me to focus more on the actual writing and cartooning, which is really all that matters.

Having said all that, these are the tools that are currently sitting beside my drafting table. They're the ones I've used for my recent *New Yorker* covers, as well as my book *The Loneliness of the Long-Distance Cartoonist*.

HB
uni
0.5
MINT
BLUE
Nano Dia
Color
erasable

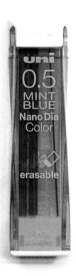

Muji Low Center Gravity mechanical pencil
Uni 0.5 mm mint blue Nano Dia lead

I use this pencil and lead for all my preparatory drawing. I like the light blue lead because it doesn't reproduce in the scanning/printing process, so I don't have to erase after creating the final line drawing in ink.* But be fore-warned: the pencil lines tend to fade fairly quickly. I'm not sure if it's just a chemical reaction with the air or if it has to do with the friction of moving your hand over the mark-ings as you draw, but I would recommend moving on to the inking phase as quickly as possible.

----

* Credit where credit is due: I started using "non-photo blue" pencils af-ter seeing Chris Ware's original pages and wanting, in some tiny way, to emulate their multi-layered beauty.

ELASTOMER ERASER
MONO zero

Tombow Mono Zero eraser
Pentel Clic Eraser

Most of the "how-to" books I read as a kid recommended either an artgum or kneaded eraser, but I always found artgum erasers to be too crumbly, and kneaded erasers too gentle. I prefer these white plastic erasers, and they seem to have grown in popularity over the years. There are also big chunky versions, but I feel like if I need to do that much erasing, I should just start over.

Also: watch out for the plastic stick embedded in the end of the Tombow eraser. If you're not paying attention, you can wear the eraser down to that point and end up scratching your artwork in a way that not only damages your drawing but also the surface of the paper.

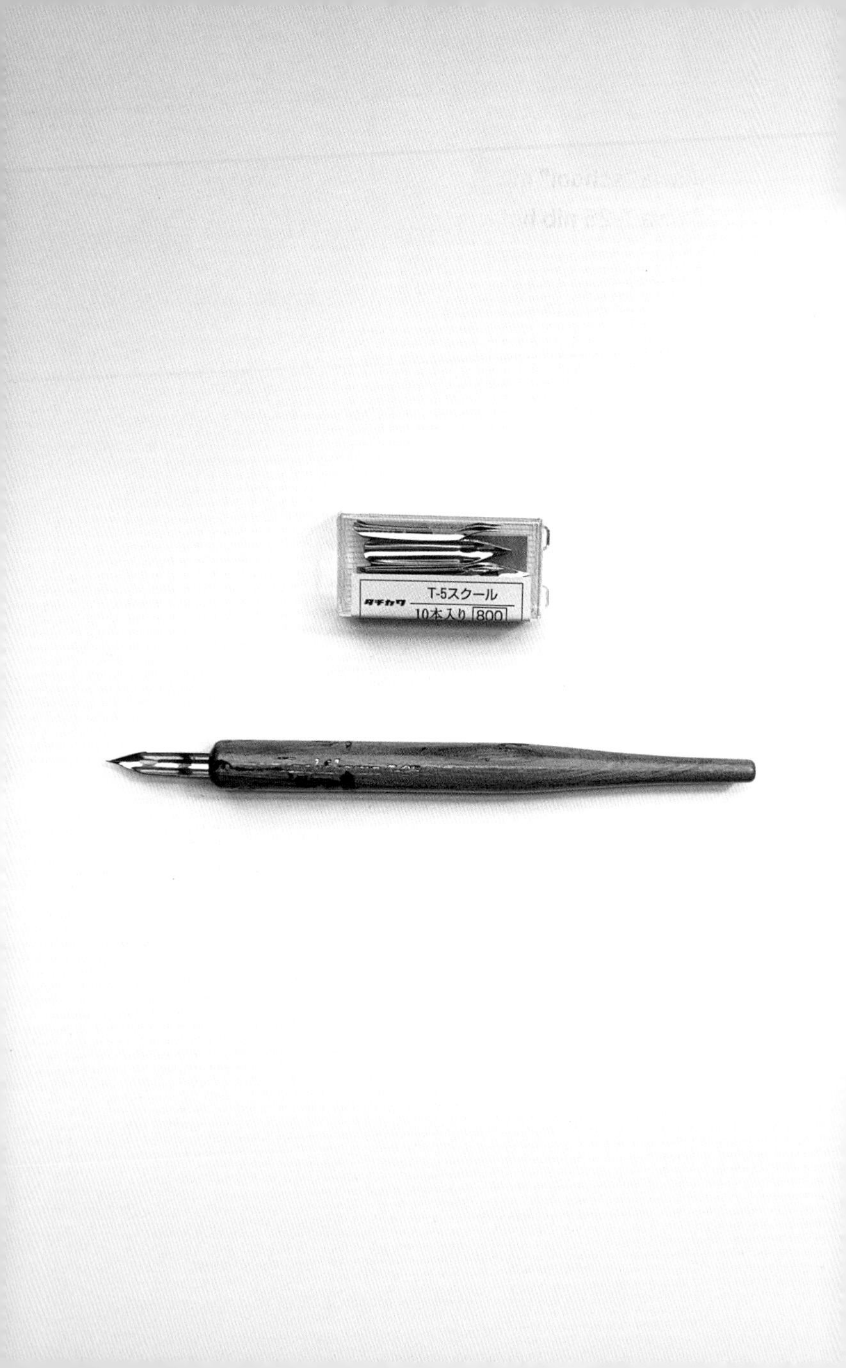

タチカワ
T-5スクール
10本入り
800

Tachikawa "school" nibs
Tachikawa T-25 nib holder

These are great pens and nibs from Japan, and now they're pretty easy to find in the US. This particular nib is nice and firm, but with just a little bit of "give" for line-width variation. A dip pen is probably the most antiquated tool I use, but I love it—not just for the line it produces, but also because it makes me feel like a real cartoonist. I used this pen for all the drawing in *The Loneliness of the Long-Distance Cartoonist*.

XS
S
M
F
FABER-CASTELL
FABER-CASTELL
FABER-CASTELL
PITT artist pen

Faber-Castell Pitt Artist Pen, sizes XS, S, F, and M

For about 20 years, I was a devoted Rapidograph* pen user, and then at a certain point I just got sick of dealing with them. They're great when they're working properly, but all the fuss of cleaning them, refilling them, having them clog right when I need them...I just got tired of it. So I started using these disposable pens instead, for things like panel borders and lettering, and I actually like them better. Unlike a Rapidograph, these have a little bit of "give," so depending on how hard you push down on them, you can get a slight line-width variation. I think it's made my lettering look a little softer and more lively.

And yes, I know that's the whole point of Rapidographs: that they deliver a steady, even line. I'm not criticizing them for that...just saying that I personally prefer the slight pressure response from the Pitt pens. And yes, I know the ink isn't as good. I get it. Everybody calm down, especially you fanatical Rapidograph zealots!

---

* For those unfamiliar, the Rapidograph is a refillable drafting or techni-cal pen with a significant number of cartoonist devotees.

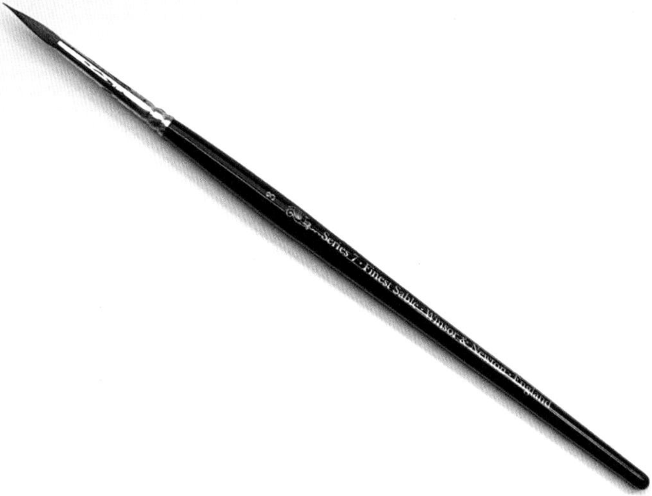
8
Series 7 · Finest Sable · Winsor & Newton · England

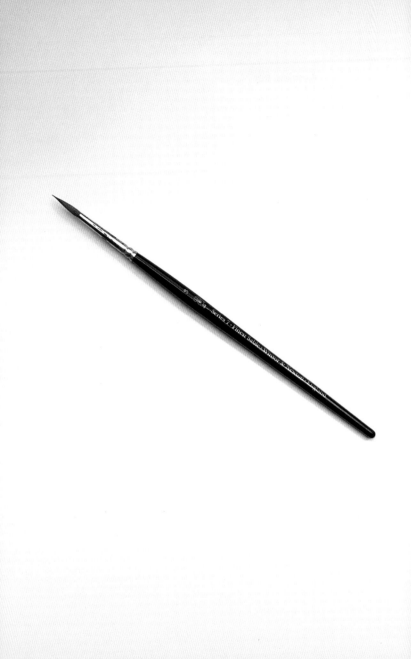

Winsor & Newton series 7 brush (size 3)

Okay, this is the one expensive, inconvenient, old-fashioned cartoonist tool that I still rely on. There's a reason why so many cartoonists use it for inking: it's dependable, versatile, and, if cared for properly, it can last a long time. I use this for the thicker, more expressive lines in my *New Yorker* covers, and for filling in black areas. If you use a slightly textured paper, you can control the roughness of the line with varying amounts of ink.

Just be sure to never let the brush dry out with ink on it. It will ruin it, and you won't be able to get a nice point from the fibers. As soon as I'm done using it, I wash the brush with water and B&J Brush Cleaner and Preserver, squeeze out any excess water with a tissue, then twirl the fibers to a point and let it dry. I told you it was inconvenient!

Dr. Ph. Martin's
SINCE 1934
TECH
DRAWING INK
14W BLACK
Dr. Ph. Martin's
SINCE 1934
TECH
DRAWING INK
14W BLACK

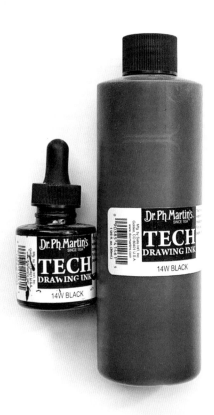

Dr. Ph. Martin's ink, either TECH or Black Star

I'm not actually sure that the black TECH ink is still available. I ordered a bunch of large bottles of the stuff years ago, and I'm still using it. But the "hi-carb" Black Star ink is a perfectly good substitute.

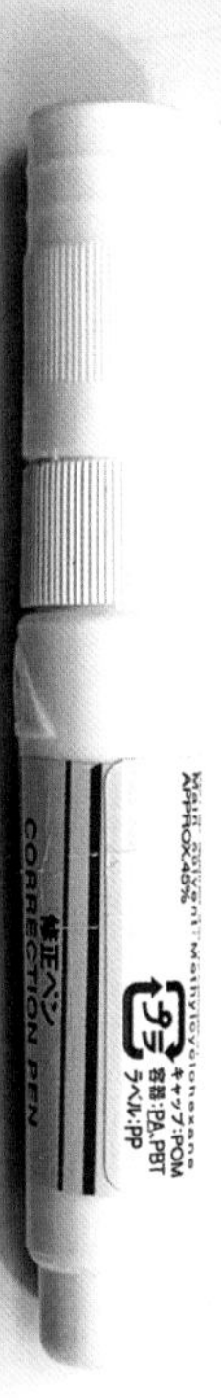
Methylcyclohexane
APPROX.45%
キャップ:POM
容器:PA,PBT
ラベル:PP
修正ペン
CORRECTION PEN

Muji correction pen

By far the best, most reliable "white-out" pen. For some reason, this one doesn't clog the way most others do, and the paint is perfect for inking over.

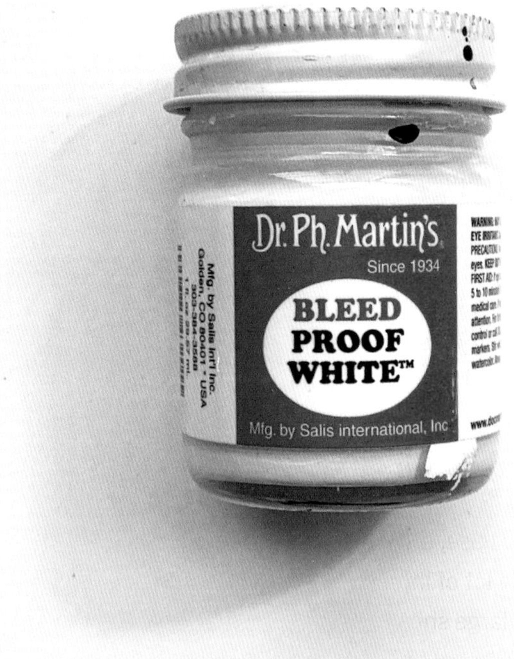
Dr. Ph. Martin's
Since 1934
BLEED PROOF WHITE™
Mfg. by Salis international, Inc

Dr. Ph. Martin's Bleedproof White

This is basically just white paint that I can dilute and apply with a brush. It allows more accuracy and texture than a correction pen, and it can create a nice rough edge for certain effects. But beware: it's water-soluble so don't try to ink over it.

(Oh, and in terms of paper, I don't have a super strong endorsement. As I mentioned, using cheap supplies can be very liberating. But sometimes, a job calls for something a little more substantial than Rite Aid printer paper. For *The Loneliness of the Long-Distance Cartoonist*, I used a brand of paper that I will not identify here by name. It's affordable, widely-available, and it worked fine for my purposes, but I just can't bring myself to endorse the insulting comics-related name and branding. If you've seen it, you probably know what I'm talking about. For *Shortcomings* and most of my *New Yorker* covers, I use Strathmore 400 Series Bristol board (4-ply, vellum surface). This is the fanciest, most expensive paper I use, and it's particularly useful for artwork that involves a lot of ink. (Lighter paper tends to buckle or rip.) I buy the large sheets (usually stored in flat files at better art supply stores) and cut them down to the size I need. It's kind of a pain in the ass, but as far as I know, it's the only way to get the 400 series/4-ply combo that I prefer.)

Q: *Your work has changed a great deal over the years (not just from when you started but much later too). Is this largely just the byproduct of doing more and more work or do you consciously take steps to improve / grow through the work or in between work? If so, how? To me, it seems like there was huge development in the look of your work in around 2010 or thereabouts. I'm most curious about that. If you agree that there was a change then, what would you say was the reason for it?*

A: For a long stretch of my early career, I think any kind of evolution in my work was really just a struggle for competency. I started self-publishing my comics when I was sixteen, and once I realized that those comics were actually being read by strangers out in the world, I felt like I was drowning while simultaneously learning how to swim. I knew that my work was being recognized for some sort of superficial proficiency—I wasn't bad *for my age*—but I certainly didn't have the experience, the vision, or the training to create the kind of work I aspired to. I was thoroughly dissatisfied with what I was producing, and I became obsessed (probably to an unhealthy degree) with making it, uh…less dissatisfying.

Unfortunately, this multi-year, hit-or-miss learning process played out in full view to the public, with each step published as an issue of *Optic Nerve*. (Drawn & Quarterly took over the publishing reins in 1995, exposing my work to an even wider audience.) I attempted a number of ill-advised stylistic experiments, and the blatant influence of various cartoonists popped up with uncomfortable frequency. I was trying to tell stories in those early comics, but more importantly, I think I was trying to teach myself how to do it better.

The period that you refer to, around 2010, coincides with something I wrote about in response to a previous question. I had just completed the final chapter of *Shortcomings*, and after working in that precise, methodical mode for nearly five years, I was eager to find a new way of making comics. I wanted to work quicker, and more importantly, I wanted to find a way back to the sense of fun and discovery I had when cartooning was just a hobby.

Part of that process was as simple as throwing out my art supplies and starting fresh. But that idea of clearing the decks also applied to how I approached writing and drawing comics, the kinds of stories I wanted to tell, and even the types of characters I was going to focus on. Prior to *Killing and Dying*, I had largely stuck to the old edict of "write what you know," focusing mainly on semi-autobiographical stories, or at least, stories that took place (literally and figuratively) in the very small world that I inhabited. My challenge to myself with *Killing and Dying* was to create characters and stories that were outside of my own direct experience, to allow each story to have its own distinct tone, and to create each story (in terms of writing process, art style, art supplies, etc.) in a totally different way. I worried that this would result in a formless, seemingly random collection, but I think to some degree the stories were all unified by my subconscious, my aesthetics, and the limits and quirks of my drawing ability.

And just to clarify, I didn't complete *Killing and Dying* and think, "Ah...mission accomplished!" I was still dissatisfied with the results, but I felt like I'd moved the needle, so to speak. At the very least, I knew I had changed my methods, and for the first time in a while, the process of making comics felt new and exciting.

One last thing on the subject of evolution: I'd be remiss if I didn't acknowledge the influence of my wife, Sarah, who's been my most candid, consistent editor and critic for the past twenty years. We'd known each other for a little while before she read any of my books, and when she did, she was complimentary, but I could tell she was sort of holding her tongue. I finally prodded her enough, and she hesitantly said something along the lines of, "It's just…you're so funny in real life." It was both a great compliment and a devastating criticism, and I instantly knew what she was getting at. I'd been so determined to present myself as a "serious" and "alternative" cartoonist—pushing back on the then-common perception of comics as junk culture for kids—that I'd eschewed anything that reeked of the kinds of comic books I'd grown up loving: color, sound effects, thought bubbles, and, yes, humor. In general, I think I had muted the emotional tone of my stories, and that was probably a safe, contrived way of avoiding sentimentality. When Sarah encouraged me to allow more of my full personality into my work, and to not worry so much about presenting a "cool" demeanor, it felt like I'd been freed from some self-imposed shackles of pretension. I think, more than anything else, it was this mental shift that allowed me to enter a new, more expansive phase in my work. I'm certain that none of my books since *Shortcomings* would exist as we know them without Sarah's profound impact on me, both as an artist and as a person.

Q: *I read in an interview that you've been doing some screenwriting. Can you talk about adapting your stories into film, or whatever it is?*

A: I have a screenwriter friend who advised me to only talk about a film project once it's been released and received positive reviews. I understand what he meant: the process is agonizingly slow and totally unpredictable, and the risk of saying something that ends up not being true is extremely high. The fact is, most scripts/projects end up not getting made, and the ones that do are usually very different from the way they were initially conceived. So with that in mind, I'll focus here on two projects I was involved in that, for the most part, meet the aforementioned criteria.

The first one is called *Les Olympiades*. It's a French film directed by Jacques Audiard, and it's based on three stories of mine: "Hawaiian Getaway," "Amber Sweet," and "Killing and Dying." The script was written by Céline Sciamma, Léa Mysius, and Audiard. It was an official selection at the 2021 Cannes Film Festival, and it was released in France on November 3, 2021. It was released in the US shortly thereafter with the somewhat unwieldy title *Paris, 13th District*.

FESTIVAL DE CANNES
2021 OFFICIAL SELECTION

A FILM BY JACQUES AUDIARD

BASED ON SHORT STORIES BY ADRIAN TOMINE

PARIS,13th
DISTRICT

"Masterly. A silvery starburst of cinematic passion and exuberance.
Lucie Zhang [gives] a joyous, star-is-born performance."

– Robbie Collin, The Telegraph

I knew from the outset that I would not be especially involved in the adaptation process on this film. After saying "no" to similar offers over the years, I agreed to this one solely because of my great admiration for the past work of the director and co-writers. I had no creative input on the film, and was largely oblivious to its production process. Essentially, I signed the contract, waited five years, and then saw the finished film.*

Watching *Les Olympiades* was among the strangest, most indelible experiences of my life. It was the first time I'd been back in a theater since the initial COVID shutdown, and I was sitting in one of my favorite Manhattan theaters at 9:00 a.m. with an audience consisting of only my wife and someone from the American distribution company. More significantly, I was watching a breathtakingly beautiful black-and-white French film in which pieces of my characters and stories are alluded to, replicated, transformed, and, in some cases, omitted. I've read, watched, and thought a lot about the process of adapting books into films, but no amount of research could've prepared me for the experience of being a small part of that process. I did my best to just get lost in the fiction of the film, to think about it solely on its own terms, but—at least for that first screening—it was impossible.

---

* I literally learned about the cast, as well as the title of the film, when its IMDb page was updated.

In some ways, I feel like *Les Olympiades* is an original work, only loosely inspired by my stories. But other people who've seen it have said the exact opposite—that it's very much an adaptation, and that it's infused throughout with aspects of my comics and illustrations—and I admit that I'm completely unable to be objective on this matter. Either way, watching the film was at once an incredibly moving, humbling, and occasionally frustrating experience for me. I will admit that, as a lifelong movie obsessive with a particular fondness for French cinema, I nearly burst into tears when I saw my name pop up in the opening credits among all those other names. I was overwhelmed by the film's energy and beauty, and I felt honored to be some small part of that unfathomable accumulation of talent and labor.

The second adaptation that has come to fruition (as of this writing) is *Shortcomings.* I was much more involved in the development of this one, and I wrote the screenplay. The film was directed by Randall Park, and it had its premiere at the 2023 Sundance Film Festival. It was an official selection at the Tribeca Festival, and was released in theaters by Sony Picture Classics on August 4, 2023.*

---

* Unfortunately, that release date landed right in the midst of the historic writers' and actors' guild strikes, so none of the cast and crew were able to do any promotion. But that's another story!

JUSTIN H. MIN   SHERRY COLA   ALLY MAKI

SHORTCOMINGS

A FILM BY RANDALL PARK
BASED ON THE GRAPHIC NOVEL BY ADRIAN TOMINE

To my great surprise, the process of adapting my comic into screenplay form was one of my all-time favorite creative experiences. At the end of a work day, my wife was often surprised by what a good mood I was in—something that was often not the case when I was midway through a 200-page graphic novel. After thirty years of making comics full-time, it felt weirdly exhilarating to simply sit at a desk instead of a drafting table, to be able to edit something with relative ease, and for once, to have work that was portable. I was able to go on family vacations and still get some real work done after the kids had gone to bed. I could be one of those guys who pretentiously sits in a café working on his screenplay.* I could change the way a character looks with a few taps of the keyboard, rather than having to arduously white-out and redraw every panel they appeared in. I also felt like it was an incredible opportunity for me to revise, update, and (hopefully) improve upon the material. To be honest, I've never been 100% satisfied with anything I've published, so the chance to take another swing at this story was something I relished.

To my even greater surprise, I actually loved the entire process of working on the movie, all the way through

---

* Okay, there's probably nothing inherently "pretentious" about this. But I still couldn't bring myself to do it.

Shortcomings: A Screenplay (2023)

production to its eventual release.* After working in isolation for essentially my entire career, it was a great pleasure and a transformative education to collaborate with so many talented people. I loved every minute I spent on set—even the unbearably hot and humid night on Staten Island. The twenty-year-old version of me would sneer at this, but I have to admit: I loved being part of a team. The goal of staying true to the source material but also aiming for something that works well in its new incarnation was a thrilling, sometimes maddening endeavor, that for now at least, feels very addictive.

---

* That's not 100% true—there were definitely periods of frustration, anxiety, and conflict, but in hindsight I'm happier to have had those experiences than not.

Q: *I'm a filmmaker and cartoonist, and I have a crazy question about [movie title redacted]. Is there any possibility of me to work on it?? I'd do anything—P.A., storyboard, even act!*

A: In recent years, this question (or some variation of it) has become the number one most common query that I receive—even outpacing the classic "How do you pronounce your last name?" I wish I could respond directly to everyone, but I'm afraid I don't have a very helpful answer. It would be amazing if I had the kind of hiring power the question implies, but to be honest, I really don't. And on top of that, I can't personally vouch for random people who reach out to me on Instagram! My suggestion would be to zero in on the one aspect of filmmaking that really interests you (or that you think you'd be good at), and then investigate and reach out to people or companies who do that kind of work. My guess is that will yield better results than reaching out to an unknown screenwriter on social media.

Q: *In terms of movies and TV, what have you been watching lately?*

A: My immediate impulse was to respond to this question by carefully curating my recent viewing history and omitting anything that I didn't like or am embarrassed to have watched or was forced to watch by my kids. But in the interest of transparency, I hereby submit an unedited, unranked, and unexplained list of everything I've watched in the past few months:

A Real Pain, Abigail's Party, Air, Barbie, Beau Is Afraid, Between the Temples, The Birds, Career Girls, Conbody VS Everybody, Couples Therapy, Curb Your Enthusiasm, Dìdi, Do the Right Thing, Dream Scenario, Exhibiting Forgiveness, Four Days in July, Full House, Fuller House, Good One, The Graduate, Grown-Ups, The Holdovers, House Hunters, Indiana Jones and the Dial of Destiny, In the Summers, Jessie, Killers of the Flower Moon, L'Argent, The Last Detail, Leo, Love Me, May December, No Hard Feelings, Nuts in May, Past Lives, Pickpocket, Ponyboi, Quiz Lady, Rope, Sansho the Bailiff, Sasquatch Sunset, Showing Up, Songs from the Second Floor, Stromboli, sMothered, Sofia the First, Stress Positions, Suncoast, Taylor Swift: The Eras Tour, Telemarketers, The Thundermans, Will & Harper, Yes Day, You Are So Not Invited to My Bat Mitzvah, You Hurt My Feelings

Q: *At the end of* The Loneliness of the Long-Distance Cartoonist, *it shows you getting out of bed, presumably to begin this very work. You get a notebook out that is much like the design of this book, and begin working. Did you illustrate this book in a notebook or was it on more traditional sheets of paper?*

A: I've been cagey about this in the past, but I guess now is as good a time as any to come clean. I wanted to create the impression that I drew the entirety of *TLOTLDC* directly into a Moleskine sketchbook, and that the published book was basically a replica of that sketchbook. But that's not actually the case. Evidently, that would've been too easy and spontaneous for me, and I had to find a way to make everything much more complicated.

I did draw very rough versions of a lot of the anecdotes in a small "squared notebook," but they were almost indecipherable to anyone other than me. It was just the quickest transcription of a real event, like the way someone might scrawl words in a diary meant for their eyes only. But the belief that no one would ever see this stuff was useful in that it allowed me to record some truly bizarre, mortifying moments—the kind of memories that are often buried or whitewashed by shame, and precisely the type of material that I wanted for this book.

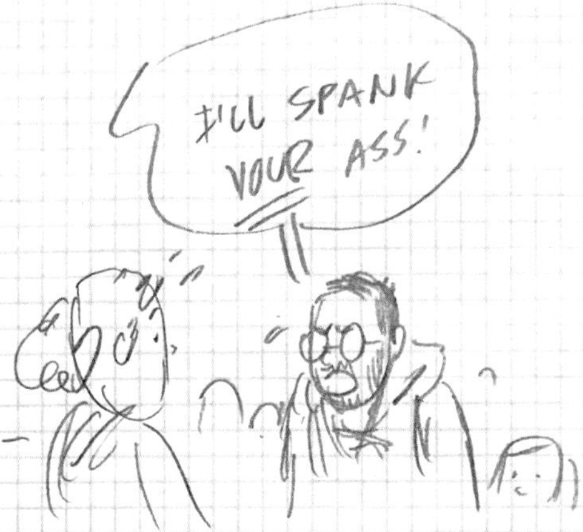
I'LL SPANK YOUR ASS!

PENN STATION, 2/12

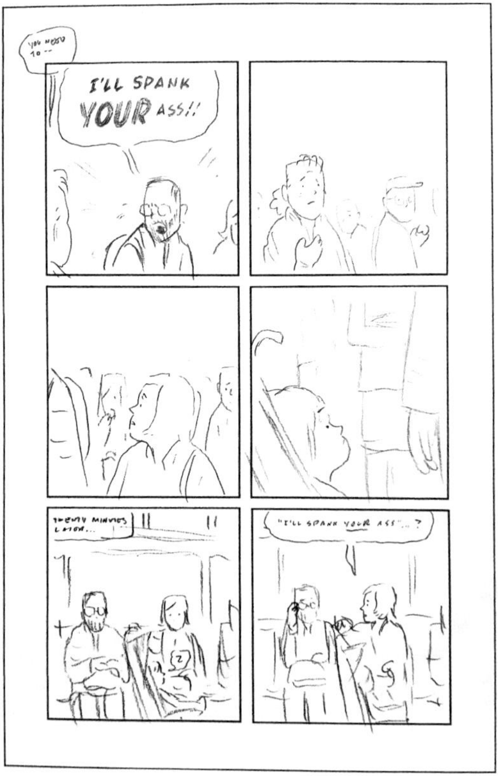
YOU NEED TO --
I'LL SPANK YOUR ASS!!
TWENTY MINUTES LATER...
"I'LL SPANK YOUR ASS"... ?

WAS I HALLUCINATING,
OR DID YOU SAY
"I'LL SPANK YOUR ASS"
TO THAT ELDERLY
HOMELESS WOMAN ?

S: SO...
A: LET'S JUST
PRETEND THAT
DIDN'T HAPPEN

When I decided to try to expand upon these scribbles and turn them into a book, I made a six-panel template in InDesign and printed out a big stack. And then I basically "wrote" the book on those printed pages, sketching out each panel very loosely in pencil, often making notes and trying out alternative ideas in the margins.

This was by far the most time-consuming part of the book's creation, and there were multiple discarded drafts of every single page. It was tempting to work out some of the dialogue in script form on the computer, but for a book that relies so heavily on facial expressions, gestures, and timing, it felt necessary to do all the writing in the language of comics.

The act of translating a real experience into comics form is sometimes a harder task than you'd expect. For me, just getting the simple facts of the story transmitted to the reader was often surprisingly difficult. I could recall these incidents in my mind perfectly, but as is often the case with memories and dreams, I saw them from a first-person point of view. I had to reimagine all of the material in a more objective, third-person mode, and that often entailed envisioning things (e.g. myself) that I couldn't have actually witnessed. Similarly, every-thing about these anecdotes made perfect sense in my

I'LL SPANK YOUR ASS!!
TEN MINUTES LATER
Z
"I'LL SPANK YOUR ASS"...?

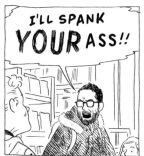

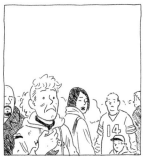

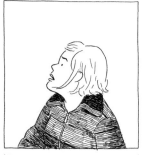

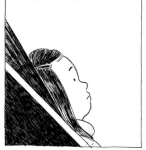

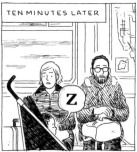

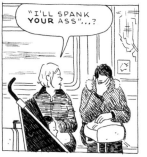

mind—any backstory or scene-setting was self-evident to me—but would often require some explanation for anyone else. I had decided early on to not use narration in this book, so any necessary information had to be expressed through "present tense" images, dialogue, or thoughts. Most of the writing process was really just me struggling to translate something that could be easily explained verbally (e.g. "I lost my mind and yelled something insane at a frail old lady, and all of Penn Station fell silent") into a sequence of clear, easily-digested panels.

The final pages were drawn on 9" x 12" Bristol board, using the tools mentioned in response to a prior question: a blue pencil, a Pitt Artist Pen, and a Tachikawa "school" nib.

The Loneliness of the Long-Distance Cartoonist (2020)

Then I scanned these pages into the computer and placed them on top of a light blue grid pattern that I created in Photoshop.

So there you go. A long, convoluted process designed to create the illusion of being quick and spontaneous. Advice to aspiring cartoonists: don't do this.

Q: *When looking at your Instagram posts that show your process of work, it would appear that you use blue pencil for sketching, ink over that, then color digitally. Why do you start traditional, then transition to digital?*

A: I'm happy to answer this question, but as with my previous response, I intend this only as an explanation of my personal working methods, not as any kind of prescriptive advice. But you're absolutely correct about my process for creating color images. It's something of an analog/digital hybrid, in which I draw all the artwork with ink on paper, and then I create the color digitally (with a weird combination of Photoshop, Illustrator, and InDesign).* Here's an example from a recent illustration for *The New Yorker*.

---

* Credit where credit is due: this method was taught to me decades ago by John Kuramoto, and it's a testament to his prescience and perfectionism that I've never found a reason to depart from his original instructions.

You might be wondering why, in the 21st century, am I still drawing on paper? The simplest explanation is that I enjoy working with pens and pencils and paper, and for whatever reason, I find working on a computer to be a physically-taxing, eyeball-straining chore. Creating the line art is the most time-consuming part of the illustration process, and I prefer to spend those hours hunched over my drawing board rather than staring into a screen. Also, over the years I've learned to draw in a physical, tactile way. The sensation of pencil, pen, and brush on paper is deeply embedded in my technique, and I delight in the unexpected marks that come from a slightly dry brush or a worn-down nib. I like being able to rotate the paper so that I can find the perfect angle for pulling a brush across the surface. As odd and fetishistic as it may sound, I enjoy making corrections by scratching away dried ink with an X-acto knife or brushing on just enough layers of semi-transparent white paint. I know, I know...this can all be digitally replicated with incredible ease. Probably true, so let's just say it's an eccentric personal preference/ mental illness and leave it at that.

So then why do I create the color on a computer? This choice is based entirely on the end results I'm trying to achieve, as well as the current printing technology that's used to reproduce my work. I want my artwork to have flat, mechanical-looking color, like the comics and illustrations I grew up studying. It might be different if I was aiming for a modeled, painterly result. In that case I could apply watercolor directly onto the line art. But ironically, a computer is the best tool for me to emulate the look of coloring that was created in the pre-digital era.

A few last thoughts about all this. Aside from the matter of personal preference, I think it's worth mentioning that drawing on paper results in tangible artwork that can be exhibited and sold. I know that sounds like I'm stating the obvious (let's spare ourselves any discussion of NFTs

for now), but it's something to consider. At the risk of sounding gauche, I think it's important to share that I've made far more income over the years from selling original artwork than I have from publication fees, advances, or royalties. If money's not a concern for you, or if you have a regular job and you're just making comics as a hobby, then don't worry about this. I understand that sometimes you need to just get the pages drawn, in as quick and easy a way as possible. But I can tell you that as a full-time cartoonist/illustrator with a family, art sales have completely saved my ass (and by extension, my family's asses) innumerable times over the years.

Adam Baumgold Gallery, November 18, 2018

Also, I got to bring my dad to a gallery show of my work here in New York before he passed away, and that's an experience that means more to me than any time I might've saved by drawing on a screen.

Q: *When writing your stories, how much prose do you produce before beginning the thumbnails or sketches?*

A: Almost none. As much as possible, I try to write comics in comics form, which allows me to think about the words and images simultaneously, as well as how a panel will interact with the other panels around it. I can say with absolute certainty that this method has led to innumerable ideas/beats/details/jokes/etc. that never would've occurred to me if I was just typing a script and then translating that script into comics form.

I will sometimes scribble out notes in advance, and every once in a while I'll type on my computer if there's a very long, convoluted piece of dialogue or narration that I need to finesse. But for the most part, this is how I've written my last couple of books: very rough pencil drawings on paper, arranged in an Itoya folder (plus a mountain of crumpled up "reject" pages on the floor).

Rough draft, *Shortcomings*, pages 72–73 (2004)

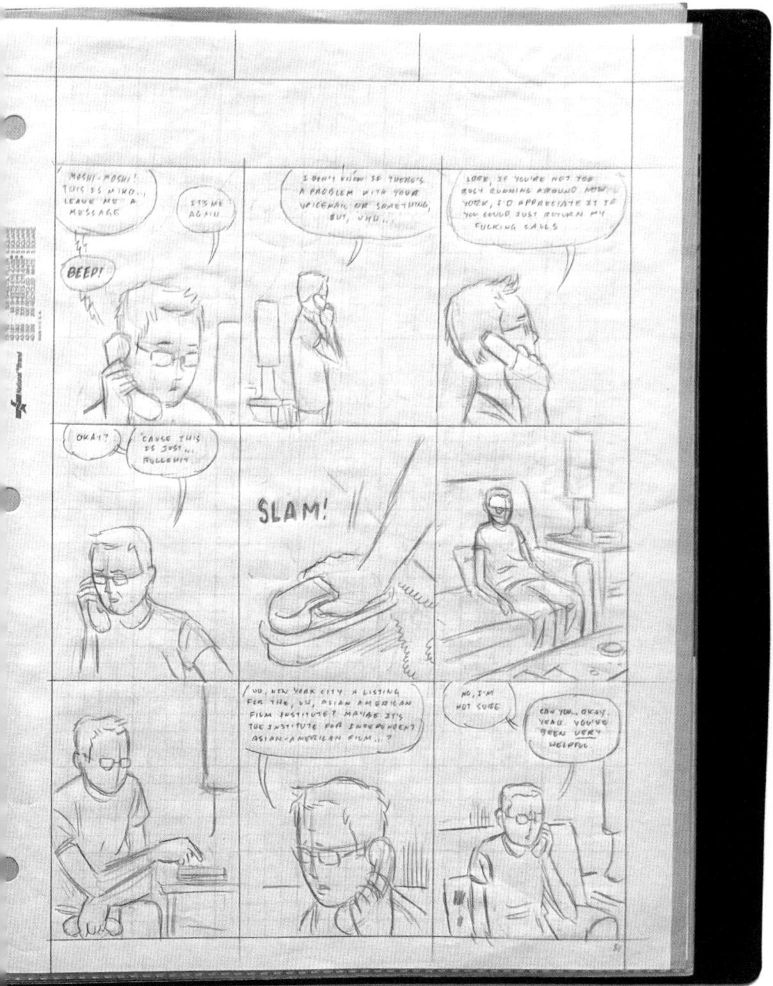
MOSHI-MOSHI! THIS IS MIKO... LEAVE ME A MESSAGE
BEEP!
IT'S ME AGAIN.
I DON'T KNOW IF THERE'S A PROBLEM WITH YOUR VOICEMAIL OR SOMETHING, BUT, UHH...
LOOK, IF YOU'RE NOT TOO BUSY RUNNING AROUND NEW YORK, I'D APPRECIATE IT IF YOU COULD JUST RETURN MY FUCKING CALLS
OKAY?
'CAUSE THIS IS JUST... BULLSHIT
SLAM!
UH, NEW YORK CITY. A LISTING FOR THE, UH, ASIAN AMERICAN FILM INSTITUTE? MAYBE IT'S THE INSTITUTE FOR INDEPENDENT ASIAN-AMERICAN FILM...?
NO, I'M NOT SURE
CAN YOU... OKAY. YEAH. YOU'VE BEEN VERY HELPFUL

Q: *What is your approach on the 180 degree rule*? Is it something you try to keep in mind as much as you can, or is it not something you consider to be important at all?*

A: I don't think about it consciously, but in my effort to make my comics as clear and readable as possible, I find I'm often intuitively obeying it. People have pointed out examples of it in my work, and I've been surprised. The truth is, my panel compositions are generally not flashy or dynamic, and it would probably require more effort on my part to violate the 180 degree rule than to respect it. Sometimes, as in this page from *Shortcomings*, the setting basically imposes the rule.

---

* A much more detailed explanation can be found online, but the 180 degree rule is a cinematic concept regarding camera placement in relation to characters on screen, and it has been adopted and discussed at length by some cartoonists and comics-related academics.

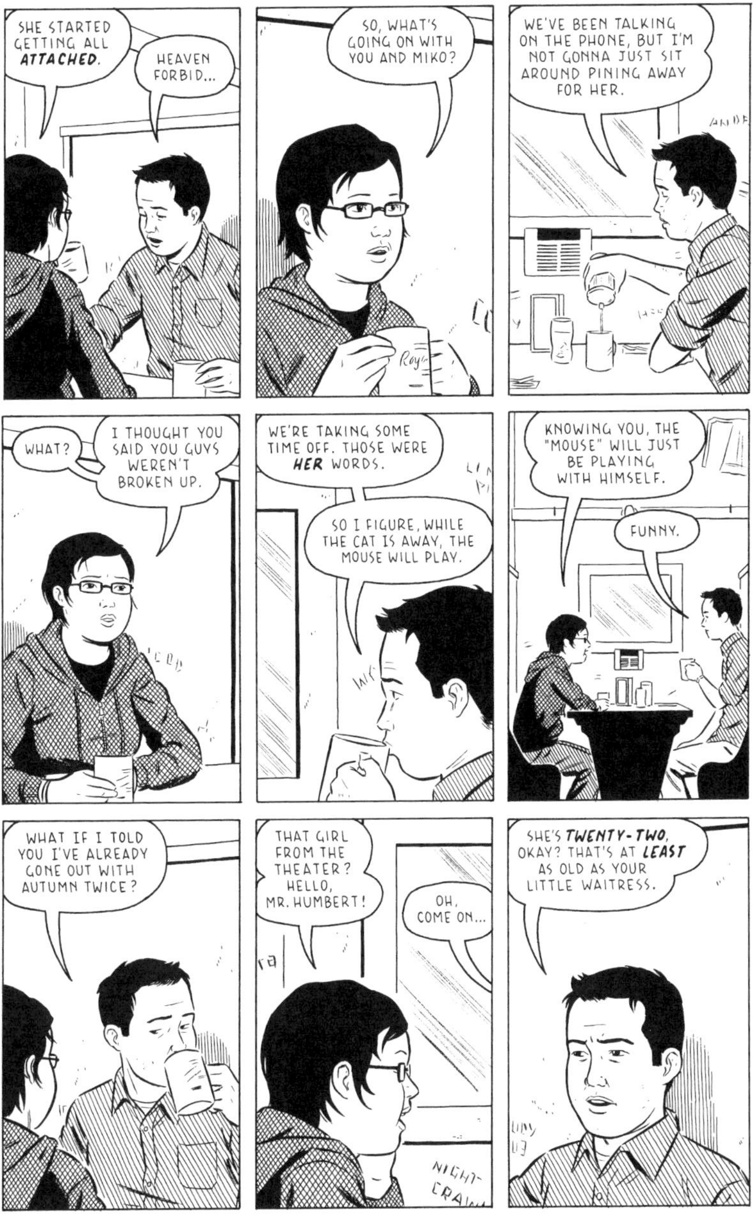
SHE STARTED GETTING ALL ATTACHED.
HEAVEN FORBID...
SO, WHAT'S GOING ON WITH YOU AND MIKO?
WE'VE BEEN TALKING ON THE PHONE, BUT I'M NOT GONNA JUST SIT AROUND PINING AWAY FOR HER.
WHAT?
I THOUGHT YOU SAID YOU GUYS WEREN'T BROKEN UP.
WE'RE TAKING SOME TIME OFF. THOSE WERE HER WORDS.
SO I FIGURE, WHILE THE CAT IS AWAY, THE MOUSE WILL PLAY.
KNOWING YOU, THE "MOUSE" WILL JUST BE PLAYING WITH HIMSELF.
FUNNY.
WHAT IF I TOLD YOU I'VE ALREADY GONE OUT WITH AUTUMN TWICE?
THAT GIRL FROM THE THEATER? HELLO, MR. HUMBERT!
OH, COME ON...
SHE'S TWENTY-TWO, OKAY? THAT'S AT LEAST AS OLD AS YOUR LITTLE WAITRESS.

Shortcomings (2007)

Q: *My question is about "pacing in comics." What's your process for "nailing down" the story's pacing per page and panel? Do you go by story beats or information you deem important, or both?*

A: I usually just try to tell the story I have in my mind, and I keep editing and adjusting the rough draft until it reads the way I want it to. For this scene from "Killing and Dying," for example, I imagined the conversation playing out in real time, and then tried to replicate that as best I could by breaking up the dialogue, expressions, and gestures into panels.

Aside from trying to make a scene feel natural and believable, the main thing I'm thinking about with regards to pacing is holding the reader's attention. I've found that too much text—regardless of how beautifully written it may be—will cause a reader to skim or skip ahead. Of course there will always be exceptions, but for a scene like this one—in which I'm basically trying to make the reader feel like they're sitting there with the characters at The Cheesecake Factory—I find that simple, easily-digestible panels with a sentence or two of dialogue work best. It might seem more economical to cram a lot of dialogue into one panel, but not only does that tend to overwhelm the reader, it gives the comic a stilted tone, as if the characters are frozen in time while reciting their pre-written words.

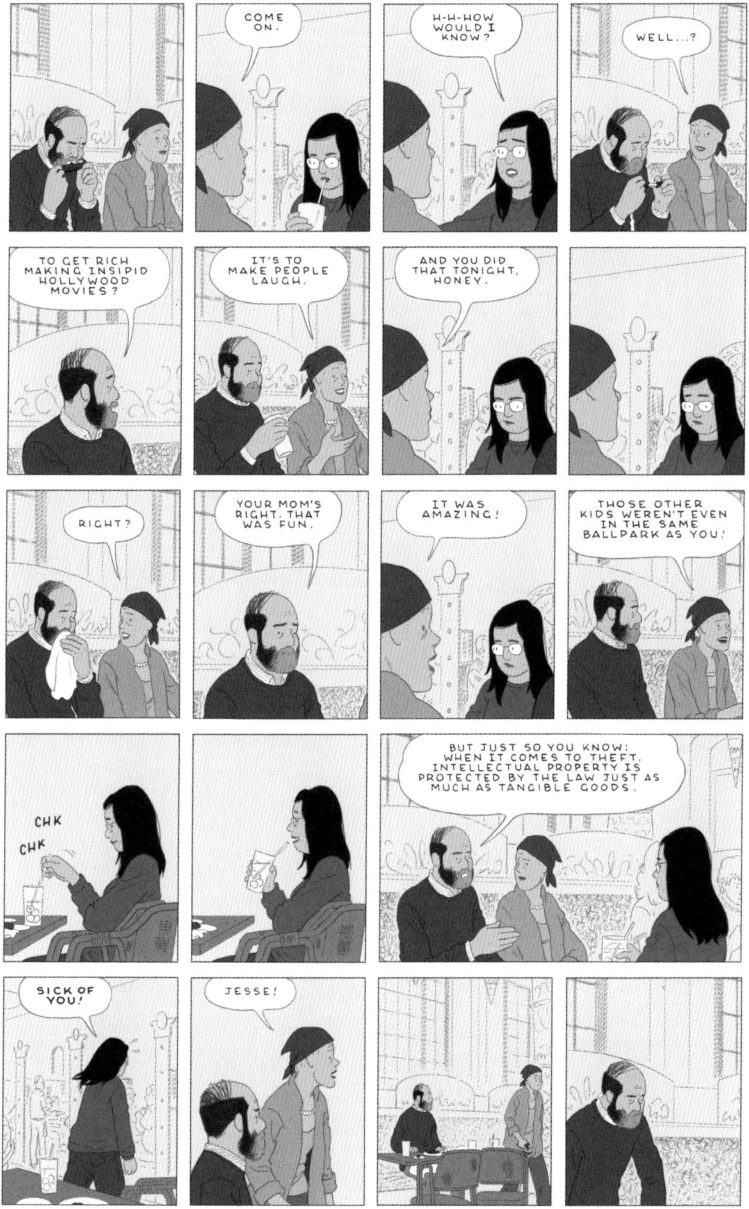
COME ON.
H-H-HOW WOULD I KNOW?
WELL...?
TO GET RICH MAKING INSIPID HOLLYWOOD MOVIES?
IT'S TO MAKE PEOPLE LAUGH.
AND YOU DID THAT TONIGHT, HONEY.
RIGHT?
YOUR MOM'S RIGHT. THAT WAS FUN.
IT WAS AMAZING!
THOSE OTHER KIDS WEREN'T EVEN IN THE SAME BALLPARK AS YOU!
CHK
CHK
BUT JUST SO YOU KNOW: WHEN IT COMES TO THEFT, INTELLECTUAL PROPERTY IS PROTECTED BY THE LAW JUST AS MUCH AS TANGIBLE GOODS.
SICK OF YOU!
JESSE!

Killing and Dying (2015)

Q: *I was wondering how often you explicitly think through how and why an ending works, versus going off a more intuitive feeling?*

A: I don't think the two approaches you describe are mutually exclusive. I give a lot of thought to my endings, but I also try to arrive at them intuitively. I know...it probably seems contradictory to say, "You should really think carefully about the ending, but don't think about it too much!" Maybe the best way to describe my approach is that I try to use my conscious mind to reject or edit the bad ideas, but I allow my subconscious mind to surprise me with the good ones.

There's a certain kind of ending that I love, and it's hard to describe, but it usually contains a mixture of surprise, mystery, simplicity, and unspoken feeling. Some of my favorite short stories by John Cheever, Raymond Carver, and Ottessa Moshfegh are good examples of this. The films *45 Years* and *The Ice Storm* come to mind. Or the original version of *The Office*. I could watch those a hundred times and still feel chills when they cut to credits. I can't really articulate why those endings have that effect on me, but that sensation is something I've thought a lot about, and have probably been chasing my whole career.

Q: *What are the most reliable methods you have found to select the moments that must be conveyed in a story, and to compose them in such a way that it affects your artistic vision?*

A: I'm not sure I completely understand your question, but I think you're assuming that I have a more strategic, methodical approach to writing than I actually do. I often start with an idea or a character or a scene, and then just let it slosh around in my brain for a long time, often while doing other things.* If I do this for long enough, I'll eventually arrive at a rough version of the complete story in my mind, and then I can finesse that to a degree as I start sketching on paper. But I usually don't have an articulated reason or explanation for why I picked each moment. I think you can usually tell when something's been written that way, and it doesn't feel very lifelike.

---

* I've basically "written" many stories while washing dishes or pushing my kid on a swing.

Q: *How do you approach writing dialogue? I have a hard time making dialogue sound unforced/genuine and move the story along.*

A: This might be a bit personal, but my sense is that people who have a hard time writing good dialogue are maybe not the best listeners. It's important to hear how other people talk, and to develop a memory bank for slang, turns of phrase, tics, trends, malaprops, and especially how and where silences land in conversations. I'm a firm believer that a writer can learn a lot by simply talking less and listening more.

On a more hands-on, practical level, when it comes to writing dialogue I think you just need to work on it— even if it means focusing on one sentence at a time— until it "sounds" the way you want it to. If it makes you feel any better, this is something that I struggle with all the time. As I described in a previous answer, I do a lot of work to make things seem like they were effortless! If you're critical of the dialogue you've written in the past, then it means you've already developed your own personal "bullshit meter." That's a big step: you're aware when something isn't right. The next step is to fix it, and the only way to do that is to try different versions of each piece of dialogue (including the version in which the dialogue is omitted completely). Sometimes this can mean something as slight as changing a single word or replacing two words with a contraction. Sometimes it can mean a major overhaul.

I find it useful to mentally (and sometimes even physically) inhabit a character—almost like I'm an actor taking on that role—and then I just speak and write in that voice. I need to feel uninhibited when I'm writing, which is why I prefer my bedroom over cafés or shared workspaces. Maybe even more importantly, I've found it helpful to let characters and stories exist and evolve and reveal themselves in my mind for as long as possible before committing them to paper. The better I know the character, the easier it is to put words in their mouth.

In terms of "moving the story along," this is where you kind of have to pull off a sleight of hand and/or be fairly ruthless. Of course it's necessary for dialogue to occasionally contain exposition or backstory or plot information, but if done clumsily, it will almost always take the reader out of the story and make them aware of you, the writer. I try to bury or obscure these tidbits as much as possible, or even cut them completely and let the reader connect the dots on their own. I wrote a story called "Intruders," and ended up whittling it down so much in the revision process that the original plot idea is only implied in a few lines of dialogue and in the relation between the first and last sentences of narration. Now, I'm sure that very few people will pick up on everything I originally had in mind with this story, but that's okay with me, and it's ultimately preferable to spelling everything out explicitly. I guess what I'm trying to say is that you might not need your dialogue to do quite as much work as you initially think.

Q: *Sometimes it takes me forever to finish a comic because I'm constantly going through phases of "this is good, ppl wanna read this" vs "wow my stuff is trash and no one will want this." Do you get phases like this? How do you stay motivated?*

A: I think you're essentially describing my base-level mental state while making comics. I honestly can't imagine going through the process of making a book with unwavering confidence and self-satisfaction. It's difficult, but I think the key to managing these kinds of conflicting thoughts is to be as objective as possible. Make sure you're not deluded in either direction, and try to evaluate your work in a way that's critical but not defeating. I also think it's useful to not obsess too much about how people will receive the work, and to instead focus on just making it as satisfying to you as possible.

Q: *Do you have any advice about how to draw somewhat realistic characters from imagination? I spent many years going to life drawing three times a week, then studied anatomy for about a year, and still, if I try to draw a figure from my head, the result looks like the demented scribbles of a child. Is there any way out of this?*

A: I think the unfortunate truth is that most people are just not able to draw quite the way they'd like to. I'm usually disappointed with my own drawings, and every single one of my cartoonist friends has expressed similar sentiments at some point. The good news is: you're interested in cartooning (I assume, since you're writing to me) and not photorealistic portraiture. There's a great history of comics in which the drawings are stylized, simplified, exaggerated, etc., and to my mind, those types of comics read much better than the ones that look like they were drawn from photographs. I'd recommend embracing and exploring the natural idiosyncrasies of your style, and perhaps focusing more on the content of your comics, not the level of slickness or realism in the drawings.

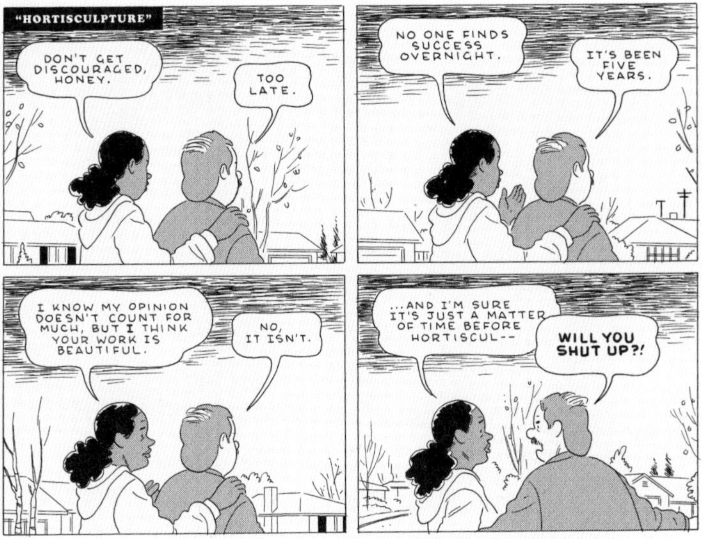
"HORTISCULPTURE"
DON'T GET DISCOURAGED, HONEY.
TOO LATE.
NO ONE FINDS SUCCESS OVERNIGHT.
IT'S BEEN FIVE YEARS.
I KNOW MY OPINION DOESN'T COUNT FOR MUCH, BUT I THINK YOUR WORK IS BEAUTIFUL.
NO, IT ISN'T.
...AND I'M SURE IT'S JUST A MATTER OF TIME BEFORE HORTISCUL--
WILL YOU SHUT UP?!

Killing and Dying (2015)

Q: *Do you ever find yourself shying away from a story you're interested in because it's either too challenging/ controversial, too far from what you think your audience is interested in, or even too close to another author's territory?*

A: I don't think I've ever scrapped a story because it was too challenging or controversial, at least not in the general sense. There were a few things I either set aside or changed because I felt that they infringed on other people's privacy (albeit in a fictionalized way). This probably wasn't the most courageous decision on a purely artistic level, but it was the right decision in terms of my relationships with friends and family.

I definitely haven't avoided a story because it was too far from what I thought my audience was interested in. I mean, I'm the guy who made a 200-page book all about his microscopic indignities in the world of alternative comics! I've talked about this elsewhere, but making comics is really too arduous of a task for me to work on anything other than something that I'm really invested in. I'm more than happy to pander in other media, but not in comics.

In terms of something being too close to another author's territory, maybe that's something I *should* be more cognizant of. But I honestly think that cartooning is such a personal, idiosyncratic art form that five people could write about the same subject matter and you'd end up with five distinct books. In fact, I'm sure that's happened.*

* Of course, this doesn't necessarily pertain to comics made by committee—there's actually thousands of those that are quite similar.

Q: *I'm an emerging cartoonist working on my first book. The pressure is killing me and dampening my natural weird story ideas and I worry the raw energy of my drawings is being lost, too. Any tips on how to keep anxiety at bay and get back in the zone?*

A: I know very well the anxiety you're describing, and I'm always struggling to find ways to minimize its presence in my own work process. For me, that often means working in secrecy. Instead of starting with a "pitch" to my publisher, I began working on my most recent graphic novel without telling anyone. I felt like I was free to explore and to make the book exactly as I wanted, and if it was horrible and I scrapped it, no one would ever know. I also didn't immediately take an advance or commit to a due date, both of which have been the source of great stress for me in the past. Of course nothing will completely eliminate feelings of pressure or anxiety, but I've found it helpful, as much as possible, to trick myself back into the mindset I had when making comics was just a hobby. It's easy to lose sight of the fact that this is something we started doing because it was fun.

The Loneliness of the Long-Distance Cartoonist (2020)

Q: *Can I ask how you got started at* The New Yorker? *I'm a long-time reader and have always been curious how one gets their work onto those pages.*

A: I'm happy to respond to this one, but I'm afraid my answer will contain very little in the way of useful information for someone hoping to find employment with *The New Yorker* now. The reason for this is that I started working for the magazine a long time ago, and almost every aspect of this story is now anachronistic, obsolete, or basically impossible. Also, I was an overconfident idiot who got a lucky break, and there's no way to be instructive in that regard. So please take this anecdote as a quaint glimpse of both my hubris and a bygone era, and not as any kind of guide to getting work at the magazine in the present day.

I didn't grow up with any connection to *The New Yorker.* In my memory, it wasn't exactly ubiquitous at the time in Fresno or Sacramento, and it certainly wasn't a fixture on my family's coffee table.* I only became aware of *The New Yorker* in my teens and early twenties—mostly through my budding interest in people like J. D. Salinger, Charles Addams, and Peter Arno—and it was probably several years later before I actually started reading it. But

---

* We were more of a *Nichi Bei Times* and *Sunset* family.

I soon became obsessed with the magazine, both in its present-day form and as a historical record of art and writing by a seemingly infinite roster of geniuses. And naturally, being the deluded, arrogant, ambitious striver that I was, I immediately thought, "I think I'd like to be a part of that!"

In 1999, I was living in Berkeley, California, and I had been working professionally as a cartoonist and illustrator for a few years, but mostly at a level that could be best described as "niche." It was around this time that I traveled to New York to visit a friend and spontaneously decided to "submit my portfolio" to *The New Yorker*. I had read about artists doing that in the old days, but I wasn't sure if it was something that people still did, and I had absolutely no idea how to go about doing it. But I had the cocky self-assurance of a 25-year-old who had already received some over-inflated approbation for his work, and that was only bolstered by the "what have I got to lose?" attitude that comes from being in a big city far from home for a few days.

The first step was assembling this so-called "portfolio." I had brought a stack of tear sheets (samples of published work, typically from magazines), but no portfolio. I had heard that some people presented their work in real portfolios—like, leather satchels with handles and flippable display pages—but when I went to the art store and saw how much they cost, I quickly decided against that. (It didn't occur to me that I might be able to retrieve the portfolio after submitting it.) So instead I went to a stationery store and bought a glossy, white, two-pocket school folder. I have no idea why I chose that particular vessel for my work, but I did. I stuffed the tear sheets into the folder, and I wrote my name, phone number, and fax number (a quaint, pre-internet mode of communication that once existed) on the front with a Sharpie. It looked like an elementary school homework assignment, and somehow I convinced myself that this was an acceptable way to present my work to one of the greatest magazines of all time.

The next step was finding out where the offices of *The New Yorker* were located. So, as one did back then, I opened up the phone book (another thing that actually once existed). I can't remember if I called *The New Yorker* and asked for their address, or if it was actually listed in the White Pages. But I eventually found it: 20 West 43rd Street.

I rode the subway down there, found the building, and walked right in. I might be mistaken, but I have no memory of any kind of security check. I took the elevator up to

The New Yorker offices, entered, and bluntly asked the receptionist, "Can I leave a portfolio?" The receptionist looked me over, probably appalled by my brashness, and responded simply, "You...can." He stretched the word "can" into two syllables, pronouncing it with a lilt that implied that, technically, it was indeed physically possible for me to leave a portfolio. At that moment I felt overwhelmed with embarrassment. Suddenly the history and dignity of my surroundings registered with me, and I felt like a small, impudent child. I pulled the stupid-looking folder out of my backpack, placed it on the reception counter, and quickly fled.

In the days that followed, I didn't think about my visit to *The New Yorker* at all. Instead I filed it away in a corner of my brain with all the other cringe-inducing mistakes of my life that I blocked out as a means of psychological survival. I eventually flew back home to Berkeley, and made a point to not tell anyone about that segment of my trip. The last thing I wanted was well-meaning friends and family continuously asking if I'd heard anything from *The New Yorker*.

But then, about three weeks later, there was a message on my answering machine (yet another thing that once existed) from someone named Chris Curry at *The New*

Yorker, asking if I was free to do an illustration that week. I played the message back several times, shaking with disbelief. I called back, and with no mention whatsoever of that glossy, white, two-pocket school folder, accepted my first assignment from *The New Yorker*. It was a small illustration of the band Luscious Jackson.

This was one of the biggest breaks of my career—clearly the result of a generous art director giving an unproven novice a chance—and...I choked. I was so overwhelmed by the significance of this one little drawing that I wound up in that illustrator's nightmare zone where the rough sketch looks infinitely better than the finished drawing, but it's literally impossible to figure out why.* More than anything, I knew I couldn't blow the deadline, so I forged ahead, adding a garish palette of colors that only made things worse. If Luscious Jackson still exists, I hereby apologize for allowing my anxiety to tarnish your spotlight moment in *The New Yorker*.

Maybe the illustration wasn't actually that bad. Or, more likely, that generous art director was even more generous than I thought. In any case, Chris kept calling me, offering me larger, more consequential assignments,

---

* Looking at it now, I can immediately point to one glaring flaw: the bizarrely tiny hands.

9

NIGHT LIFE

CONCERTS

Eric Clapton and Friends—Bob Dylan, Mary J. Blige, Sheryl Crow, and D'Angelo join Old Slowhand for an evening of guitar-hero lullabies. A benefit concert. (Madison Square Garden. 465-6000. June 30 at 7:30.)

Ann and Nancy Wilson—The singing sisters, formerly of Heart, return to give their neo-Zeppelin rock an acoustic-flavored makeover. (Beacon Theatre, Broadway at 74th St. 496-7070. June 30 at 8.)

Midsummer Night Swing—Dancing under the stars at Lincoln Center. June 30: The Gerard Carelli Orchestra and Bob Rotunda's Stardusters Big Band.... ¶ July 1: The Duke Robillard Band.... ¶ July 2: Linda Clifford and Carol Douglas lead a night of the Hustle.... ¶ July 3 at 8:15: Hemingway saw **Orquesta Aragón** play at the Tropicana during the nineteen-fifties, in Batista's Havana. Like some miraculously preserved V-8 wonder from the era of rum cocktails, cigars, and hard-swinging cha-cha-cha, this celebrated and beloved *charanga* band keeps on cruising.... ¶ July 4: D.j. Felix Hernandez, of WBGO, presents his Rhythm Revue.... ¶ July 6: Tommy Mara, with Joe Battaglia and the New York Swing Band. (Dance lessons are given each evening at 6:30; performances start at 8:15. For more information, call 875-5766.)

Central Park SummerStage—Live music in New York City's back yard. July 1 at 7:30: "**Joni's Jazz.**" With an ego as big as Malibu Beach and a tiresome persecution complex, Joni Mitchell makes it tough to love her these days. Her work speaks for itself, though, particularly the sixties and seventies albums that cut a glorious swath, from confessional folk to sleek pop to jazz-inflected art songs. Mitchell went fully electric much later than Dylan, taking the plunge with "Court and Spark" in 1974. The albums that followed, including "The Hissing of Summer Lawns," "Hejira" (featuring brilliant work from bassist Jaco Pastorius), "Don Juan's Reckless Daughter," and "Mingus," each with a deeply personal poetic voice and a broadening of musical boundaries, have turned out to be some of her most influential. For this benefit concert, a dizzying range of artists—from Duncan Shiek, PM Dawn, Chaka Khan, Jane Siberry, and Holly Cole to Ravi Coltrane, Eric Anderson, Joe Jackson, Annie Ross, Jon Hendricks, and Vernon Reid—revisit these prescient albums.... ¶ July 4 at 3: Now a trio (following the recent departure of keyboardist Vivian Trimble), **Luscious Jackson**, the band named after an obscure Philadelphia 76ers basketball player, tries to recapture the minor glory of its 1996 album, "Fever In Fever Out," which produced the hit single "Naked Eye." On the new "Electric Honey," bassist Jill Cunniff, guitarist Gabrielle Glaser, and former Beastie Boys drummer Kate Schellenbach get a little help with guest appearances from Deborah Harry and Emmylou Harris. With the Elvis-on-acid sounds of **Joh Spencer Blues Explosion** and Beastie Boys d.j. **Mix Master Mike**. (Rumsey Playfield, mid-Park at 72nd St. 360-2777.)

Tom Petty and the Heartbreakers / Lucinda Williams—Although his almost effortlessly excellent new album, "Echo," hasn't exactly galvanized the masses, Petty and his longtime lieutenants remain undeterred as they embark on yet another tour to show the whippersnappers how it's done. Williams, a forty-five-year-old unfashionable, unglamorous songwriter from Baton Rouge, is the spiritual daughter of Robert Johnson and Howlin' Wolf. She's still touring in support of her fine album "Car Wheels on a Gravel Road." (Jones Beach. 516-221-1000. July 2-3 at 8.)

Dr. John / Southside Johnny and the Asbury Jukes—A free concert by the gruff-throated New Orleans pianist and the occasional Bruce Springsteen crony. (Battery Park. No tickets necessary. July 4 at 3:30.)

Cher—Thanks to the tacky, if unbelievably irresistible, disco smash "Believe," Cher now enjoys full-metal diva status again. Her recent VH-1 appearance signalled her return to the rarefied world inhabited by such de-luxe divas as Tina Turner and Elton John. With the eighties relic Cyndi Lauper. (Jones Beach. July 5-6 at 7:30.)

CLUBS

(A highly arbitrary listing, in which boldface type indicates some of the more notable performers in town. Musicians and night-clubs proprietors live complicated lives; it's advisable to call ahead to confirm engagements.)

Arlene Grocery, 95 Stanton St., between Ludlow and Orchard Sts. (358-1633)—A narrow, dimly lit renovated bodega that's the ideal environment for three to five unknown bands a night struggling their way out of obscurity.

Bottom Line, 15 W. 4th St., at Mercer St. (228-6300)—July 1-2: Seventy-year-old **June Carter Cash**, one of the daughters of country music's first family, has just released "Press On," only her second solo album in a career that began in the Depression. Packed with classic country songs, including "Ring of Fire" (which she co-wrote with her husband, Johnny, in 1963), it is an austere collection deeply rooted in the front porches of Appalachia but leavened with a good dose of humor, evident in a song about Quentin Tarantino. She's put together a new band that includes her son John Carter Cash, and these live shows are certain to be a grand ole time.

Bowery Ballroom, 6 Delancey St. (533-2111)—June 30-July 1: Local swamp-rockers **The Bogmen.**

Chicago B.L.U.E.S., 73 Eighth Ave., at 13th St. (924-9755)—July 1: The sharp, scratchy guitar of veteran **Hubert Sumlin**, who played in Howlin' Wolf's band for twenty years.

Connolly's, 14 E. 47th St. (867-3767)—Home on Saturday nights to the rollicking **Black 47**, led by the tradition-rattling Celtic-music gadfly Larry Kirwan.

Fez, 380 Lafayette St. (533-7000)—July 4: Thirteen years ago in Oxford, England,

singer Amelia Fletcher and her brother Matthew, who played drums, formed a short-lived band called Talulah Gosh and turned out some incredible pop confections. A few years later the pair created the quintet Heavenly, which delivered more of the same sweets. It all came to an abrupt halt, however, in 1996, when Matthew committed suicide. **Marine Research**, which consists of the players from Heavenly plus a new drummer, represents Amelia Fletcher's return to the world of smart bubble-gum pop. To judge from its forthcoming album, "Sounds from the Gulf Stream," she hasn't

lost any of her shine. The **Mingus Big Band** still packs them in every Thursday. Dining.

Irving Plaza, 17 Irving Pl., at 15th St. (777-6800)—June 30: Former Clash guitarist and vocalist **Joe Strummer** has banged together a new band, the Mescaleros, and they've been touring around the U.K. for the past few months. Advance word reports a tight show of new material this upcoming single "Yalla Yalla" shows that his voice is still in good shape and that he's keeping his beats up to date) laced with Clash hits.... ¶ The Swing Dance Society gathers here every Sunday, with sets from eight until midnight. For information on the society, call 696-9737.

Knitting Factory, 74 Leonard St., between Broadway and Church St. (219-3055)—June 30: The Brazilian guitarist **Vinicius Cantuária** has lived in New York City for the past five years, and rubbing elbows with such local musicians as Bill Frisell, Arto Lindsay, and Laurie Anderson (all of whom contribute to his latest album, "Tucumã") has helped stretch bossa nova to include sampling and other technological tricks. Not that Cantuária needs much creative help; he's written hit songs for Caetano Veloso, Gal Costa, and other Brazilian superstars. The result is a sophisticated and poignant sound, full of both the excitement of being an expatriate and an intense longing for his homeland. He's joined by trumpeter **Michael Leonhart** and percussionist **Paulo Braga**. July 1: Cure alums **Lol Tolhurst** and **Andy Anderson** break out their new band, Levinhurst, in an evening of reminiscence and new music. July 2: The Japanese quartet **Melt Banana** specializes in hard-core noise, and the title of its new release (on John Zorn's Tzadik label), "MxBx 1998/13,000 Miles at Light Velocity," nicely captures its high-speed style. **Maxwell's**, 1039 Washington St., Hoboken (201-798-0406)—June 30: Even in a world made safe for pop punk by the likes of Green Day and the Offspring, **Face to Face** isn't likely to quit mixing the raw energy of screaming guitars and thumping drums with the sweetness of catchy hooks anytime soon. They've been at it for the better part of a

Luscious Jackson, at Central Park SummerStage.

decade, and their upcoming release, "Ignorance Is Bliss," lives up to its title.

Mercury Lounge, 217 E. Houston St. (260-4700)—July 1: **Face to Face** (see Maxwell's).

S.O.B.'s, 204 Varick St., at W. Houston St. (243-4940)—June 30: **Sun Ra Arkestra**. The maestro has returned to Saturn, but his band plays on. The unexpected is still to be expected. July 1: **Basement Bhangra**, an evening of ecstatic, futuristic dance music which fuses an ancient Punjabi harvest festival with the technological wonders of underground London. The d.j.s Rekkha and Joy spice the infectious dohl drumbeat with

The New Yorker (July 5, 1999)

and we began to develop a friendly, highly-efficient working relationship. On one occasion, due to some sort of tech-related conundrum that prevented me from transmitting a sketch to her, I described a revision over the phone, and she said, "Okay, I trust you."

I also began receiving assignments from another art director named Owen Phillips. He gave me my first ongoing "gig": three small images every month for the "Goings On About Town" section. It was a great assignment that not only pushed me to create images outside of my comfort zone, but also provided me with a dependable source of income right as I took the leap and moved to New York. Owen was also adamant about getting my comics into the pages of the magazine, and it was with his help that this occurred for the first time, with a piece entitled "My Ex-Barber."

In 2004, *The New Yorker*'s arts editor, Françoise Mouly, reached out to me and asked if I'd be interested in drawing a cover. True to form, I sabotaged this incredible opportunity by saying "yes" and then failing to submit any ideas. For a long time. Once again, I was intimidated and overwhelmed to the point of paralysis. But instead of throwing up her hands and rightfully scratching me off her list, Françoise worked with me. She took an

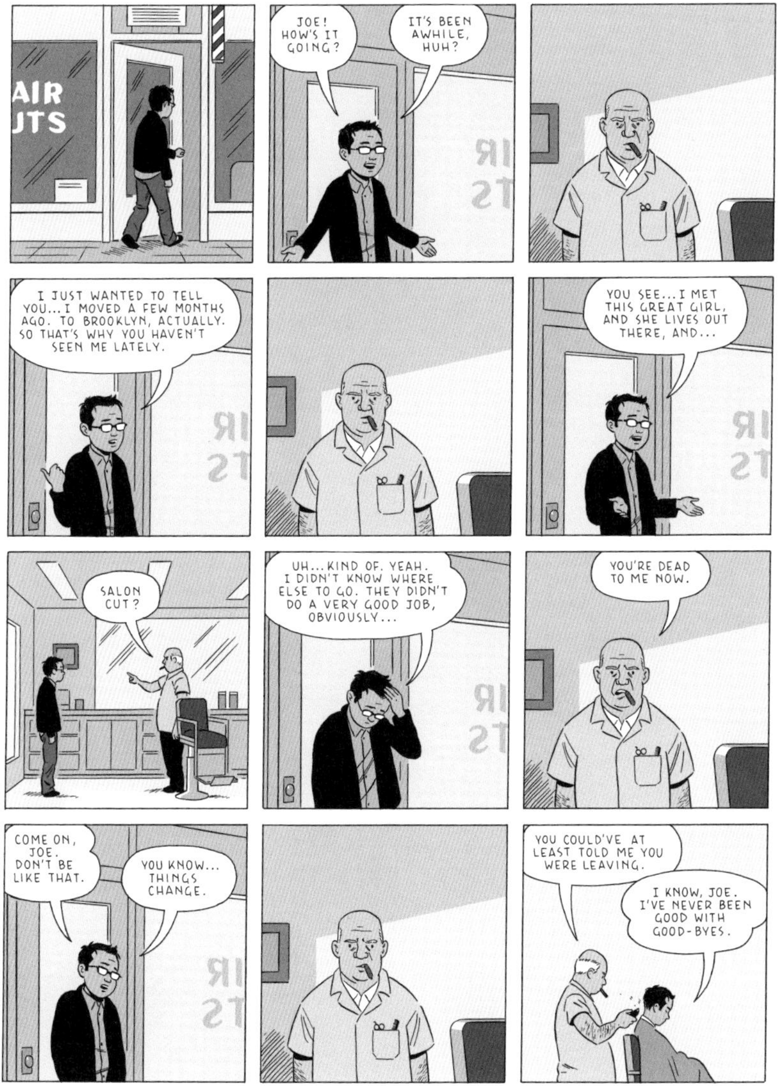
AIR
JTS
JOE! HOW'S IT GOING?
IT'S BEEN AWHILE, HUH?
I JUST WANTED TO TELL YOU... I MOVED A FEW MONTHS AGO. TO BROOKLYN, ACTUALLY. SO THAT'S WHY YOU HAVEN'T SEEN ME LATELY.
YOU SEE... I MET THIS GREAT GIRL, AND SHE LIVES OUT THERE, AND...
SALON CUT?
UH... KIND OF. YEAH. I DIDN'T KNOW WHERE ELSE TO GO. THEY DIDN'T DO A VERY GOOD JOB, OBVIOUSLY...
YOU'RE DEAD TO ME NOW.
COME ON, JOE. DON'T BE LIKE THAT.
YOU KNOW... THINGS CHANGE.
YOU COULD'VE AT LEAST TOLD ME YOU WERE LEAVING.
I KNOW, JOE. I'VE NEVER BEEN GOOD WITH GOOD-BYES.

The New Yorker (May 2, 2005)

unreasonable amount of time to walk me through the process, to encourage and advise me, and to finally apply a little "tough love" and insist that I submit some sketches by a certain date. My first cover appeared on the magazine on November 8, 2004.

It's been over twenty years since that tiny-handed image of Luscious Jackson appeared in *The New Yorker*, and I've drawn over 150 covers, comics, and illustrations for the magazine since then. It's hard for me to get my head around the fact that I've been doing this for almost half my life. Recently, I've produced work for them with less frequency because I've been engulfed in several un-predictable long-term projects, and I'm often unable to meet the deadlines of a weekly publication. But it's still my favorite magazine and my favorite place to freelance, and every time my artwork appears in its pages, I still have a flash of the exhilarating discomfort I felt when I placed that glossy, white, two-pocket school folder on the reception desk and pretended like I didn't care if any-thing came of it.

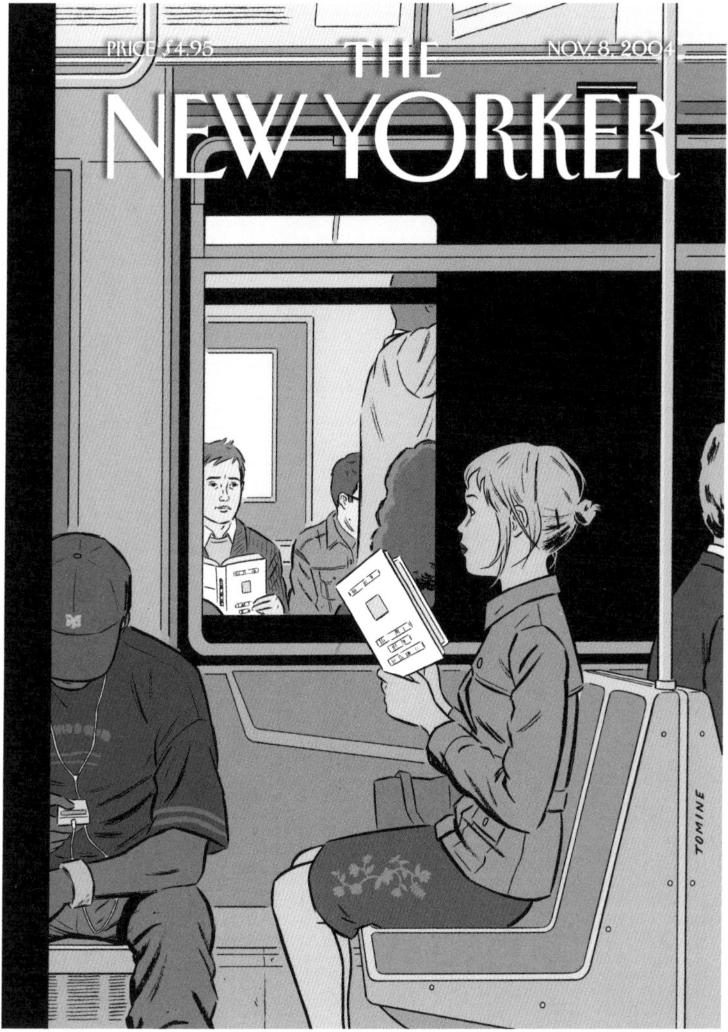
PRICE $4.95
THE NEW YORKER
NOV. 8, 2004
TOMINE

Q: *Can you please share a detailed "step-by-step" about making a cover for* The New Yorker?

A: The first step in the process is an intangible, invisible one. It's basically just me going about the normal, boring activities of my life, and then seeing or hearing or thinking about something that might be the germ of an idea. I've talked about this a little bit in relation to writing, but I will go to absurd lengths to avoid sitting down in front of a blank sheet of paper without at least a vague plan of action. I know some people are energized by that experience, but to me it's intimidating, miserable, and rarely productive.

So in this case, I didn't have to look too far for the initial idea. In the fall of 2020, most of us were living some version of this dual life where our onscreen presentation was much more carefully groomed and curated and well-lit than the chaos that existed just outside the frame. But that's all I started with: a broad, situational concept that I would need to condense into a single image. Of course, the focus would have to be on someone using a computer, and early possibilities included a kid attending online school, a family connecting with distant loved ones, and a psychologist steadfastly working with a patient. Somehow I finally settled on a young, single person on a Zoom date.

Not only did it seem like a premise that I could communicate simply and clearly, I had the sense that it might allow a tiny glimmer of much-needed levity and even—dare I say it?—uplift.

This first sketch was drawn fairly small, about 6" x 8", with a Pitt Artist Pen and a Pentel Pocket Brush. The basic composition and most of the significant details are there already, but the perspective and proportions are clearly way off.

It wasn't a conscious choice, but the vague echo of Eustace Tilley, the character depicted by Rea Irvin on the very first cover of *The New Yorker*, was immediately apparent to me. I didn't feel like I needed to draw attention to it, but I also didn't feel the need to eradicate it. The history of the magazine is something I've thought a lot about, and it seemed appropriate to leave that subconscious allusion intact.

I submitted the sketch, via email, to *The New Yorker*'s arts editor Françoise Mouly and the associate covers editor Genevieve Bormes. Françoise let me know that she liked the idea, but asked if I could revise the sketch to clarify the image's focus, perhaps with color or lighting. As usual, her note was on point, and a simple alteration (an addition, really) improved the image immensely.

I added a grey tone (and the highlights) very quickly in Photoshop, with just enough care to roughly indicate the shadows and light sources. A black-and-white image was sufficient here, as *The New Yorker* has, amazingly, always been very trusting with regards to my coloring, and I've never received a note about it.

At this point, the image was approved by both Françoise and editor David Remnick, and I moved on to creating the final image.

I drew this much larger than the sketch, which allowed a greater level of detail. I used a 13" x 16" sheet of Canson Montval watercolor paper, and I drew the image with Uni 0.5 mm mint blue Nano Dia lead in a Muji Low Center Gravity mechanical pencil.

For this version, I worked out the perspective properly (rather than just eyeballing it, as I did in the sketch). I picked a vanishing point, which you can see in the form of a small "x" on the woman's shirt, and used that as an anchor for all the lines that seem to extend out of the image towards the viewer. That's probably a confusing, clumsy way of describing this aspect of perspective. I'm sorry... just look up "perspective" or "vanishing point" and someone smarter than me can explain it!

In the penciling stage, I also added and refined a lot of the details. I improved the kitchen layout, and generally made all the clutter more specific and accurate. I added a Zojirushi rice cooker, a litter box, some hand weights, a bag of Flamin' Hot Cheetos, and a certain graphic novel that had recently been published. For most of these items, I didn't need to look beyond my immediate surroundings for reference.

I knew I wanted some kind of artwork above the bed, and I settled on a Hilma af Klint print. In my memory, the retrospective of her work at the Guggenheim was one of the last big, citywide cultural phenomenons before everything shut down, and I imagined a whole backstory about the character in my illustration attending that show with friends, purchasing the poster, and suddenly viewing it as a souvenir from a bygone era. Similarly, I decided to add to the clutter by including a discarded plastic bag (which the Chinese take-out on the table had been delivered in). The great graphic designer Milton Glaser had recently passed away, and the ubiquitous, iconic "I ❤ NY" logo on the bag was a tiny nod to his legacy. I know—it's totally insane to think about throwaway details to this degree, but I can't help but approach an illustration like this with the mind of a cartoonist, and suddenly there's a reason or a story for everything.

Once the pencil drawing was complete, I moved on to the ink phase.

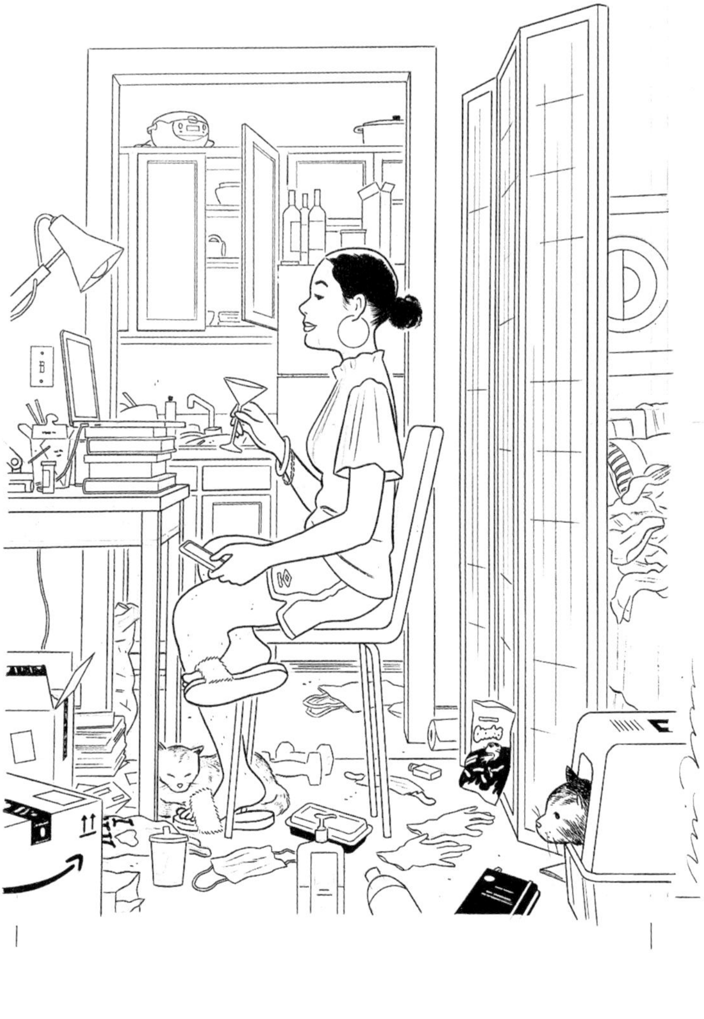

I used a Winsor & Newton series 7 (size 3) brush for anything that looks soft, fuzzy, or squishy (e.g. clothing, cats, hair, pillows, masks). The sharper, more uniform lines were drawn with either a Pitt Artist Pen or a Tachikawa "school" nib. Touch-ups and alterations (like the bottom edge of the tabletop) were made with a Muji correction pen.

Once the inking was complete, I scanned the image into the computer, creating a 1200 dpi bitmap file.

I scaled the image down to print size (7 ⅞" x 10 ¾") and made a few minor touch-ups and corrections in Photoshop.

Then I imported that image into Illustrator and created all the color. This was the step that really had me tearing my hair out. It's hard enough for me to arrive at a color scheme that just looks nice, but I was juggling a few other objectives with this one. I wanted to portray a darkened room, lit only by the lamp and the computer and phone screens (per Françoise's note), and I also wanted a sense of depth. There were a bunch of details that dictated their own palettes (like the Purell bottle, the paper coffee cup, the poster, etc.), and I wanted to be as accurate as possible. And most of all, I wanted all the colors to somehow look eye-catching and pleasant, with the right balance of

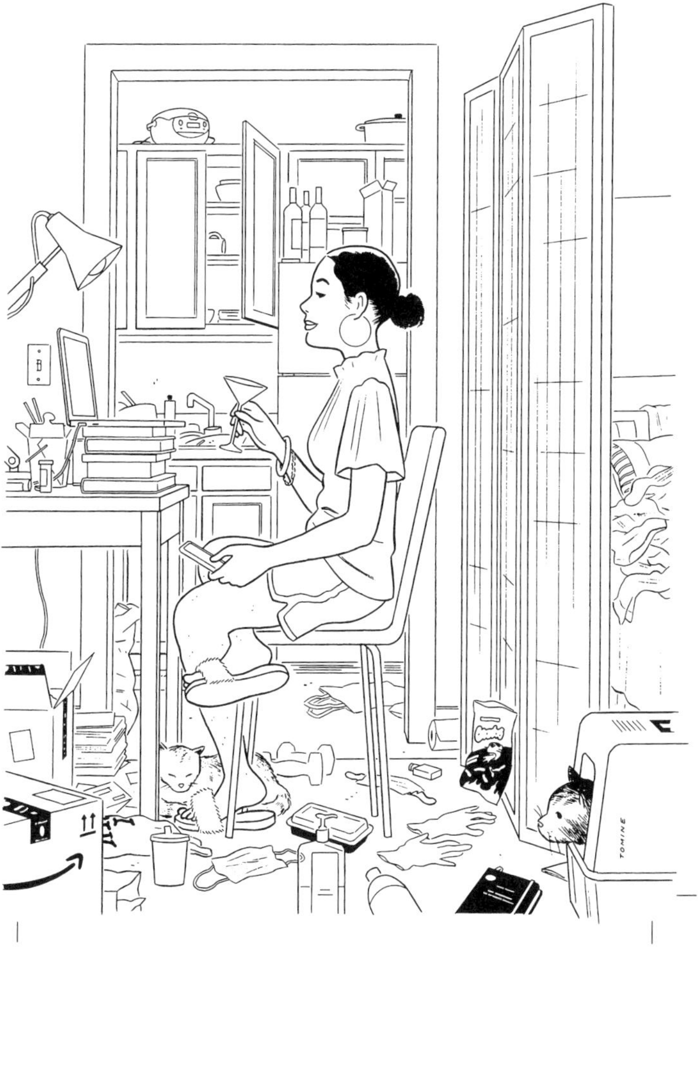
TOMINE

harmony and contrast. In the end, it was a matter of com-promising on all those fronts, and eventually arriving at the best version of "good enough."

The final image, including the logo and the "strap" (the band of color on the left edge), was assembled in InDesign. And that's it. I saved the whole image as a PDF and emailed it to Françoise and Genevieve.

One thing that still astonishes me about working for *The New Yorker* is that I can turn in an illustration on Thursday, and by Monday, it's everywhere: on news-stands, online, in people's hands on the subway, and even, in this case, on daytime TV.* There's no other ven-ue for my work that gets a quicker or bigger response (or impresses my Brooklyn-born in-laws more), and for that week or so after a cover is published, I kind of feel like a big deal. And then I go back to being a cartoonist.

---

* This particular cover was shown and discussed, for some reason, on *The View.*

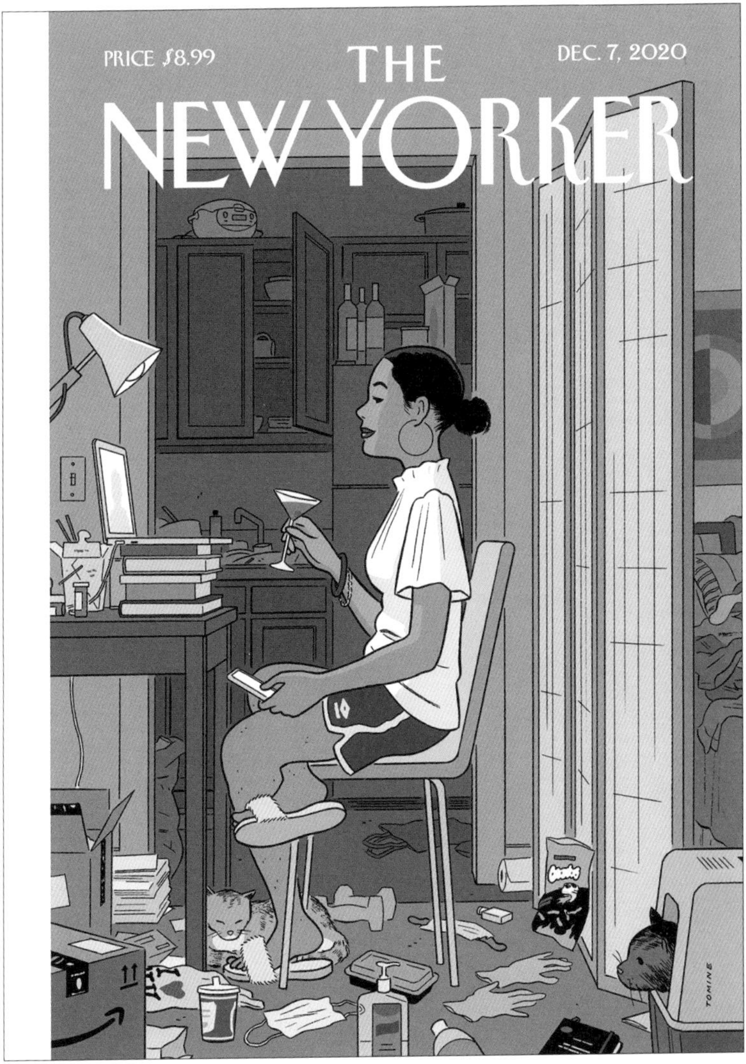
PRICE $8.99
THE NEW YORKER
DEC. 7, 2020
TOMINE

Q: *Who was the first cartoonist you ever met?*

A: Morrie Turner, creator of the comic strip *Wee Pals*. I took a summer school class from him in Sacramento when I was a kid, and he was incredibly generous and encouraging. At the end of the summer, my dad invited him over to our house for lunch, and he accepted. I remember that we had dim sum, and it felt (to me) like a celebrity had graced us with his presence. I really loved talking to him.

Q: *Please talk about how being a parent affects your art and process!*

A: I've written and talked a lot about how becoming a parent has had such a profound, positive impact on me as an artist. In a 2018 interview with *The Washington Post*, I said, "When I finished my previous book, *Shortcomings*, I honestly felt like I'd painted myself into a corner in terms of subject matter and tone and style, and I was kind of stumped about how to escape. And having kids was like discovering this secret trap door in that corner that allowed me to write differently about new things. It's also just had such a strong impact on me as a person, especially in terms of how I interact with the world, that I think that can't not show up in the work to some degree."

I still stand by all the positive things I wrote and said on this topic over the years, but I also wish I'd been a little more nuanced. I see so many interviews with artists and writers and especially celebrities who rhapsodize about parenthood, and I never feel like they're being 100% honest. I don't like the idea of some new parent struggling to create artwork and thinking, "Why the fuck is it so easy and wonderful and inspiring for everyone else?" So as an addendum to everything I've said before, I'll also say, simply, that having kids has made it much harder for me to be an artist. There are many ways in which the two endeavors influence and enrich each other, but there's also no getting around the fact that there are a lot of demands in terms of time, energy, emotion, and finances that just didn't exist before my kids came along. Of course, I vastly prefer my life now, but I'm also very grateful to have had those luxurious years before.

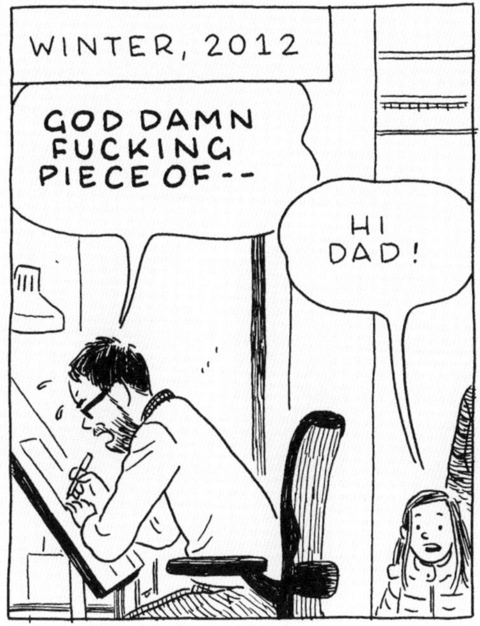
WINTER, 2012
GOD DAMN FUCKING PIECE OF--
HI DAD!

Optic Nerve #13 (2013)

Q: *What did your kids think about their appearances in* The Loneliness of the Long-Distance Cartoonist*?*

A: My older daughter read the book as I completed each page, and her interest definitely increased once she appeared as a character. But aside from a little bit of nit-picky fact-checking, she didn't say much about it until after the book was published. We were walking somewhere and, out of the blue, she said, "I read your book again last night." I asked what she thought of it, and she replied, "It was kind of funny but also sad." I asked what was sad about it, and after a long pause, she said, "I always thought you liked *The Greatest Showman*."* And then she changed the subject.

My other daughter is too young to read it, but she's looked at it. Apparently one day at school she told her teacher and classmates, "My mom is a doctor who helps people with their feelings, and my dad sits at home and draws pictures of himself."

_____

*There's one line in the book that vaguely implies the contrary.

Q: *I saw a photo of your studio online. What make and model is your drafting table?*

A: It's just an Alvin drafting table that I bought at Blick when I first moved to New York. I don't think there's anything particularly special about it, but it was cheap and it's held up well. I prefer the look of a wooden table, but the weird, specific reason I like these tables with white melamine surfaces is that I can draw perspective vanishing points way beyond the edge of my paper and then just erase those pencil marks with ease.

Oh no...I just looked up the drafting table online and discovered that the company went out of business! Suddenly, the thought of not being able to replace it makes the table seem a lot more precious. Maybe I should rewrite this answer and say, "It's a very rare, early-2000s Alvin drafting table..."

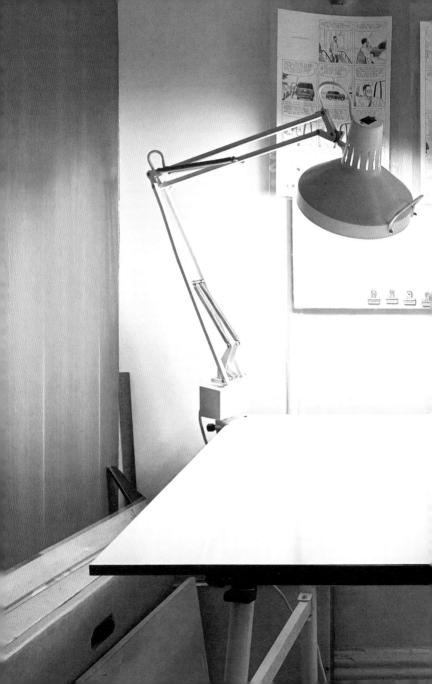

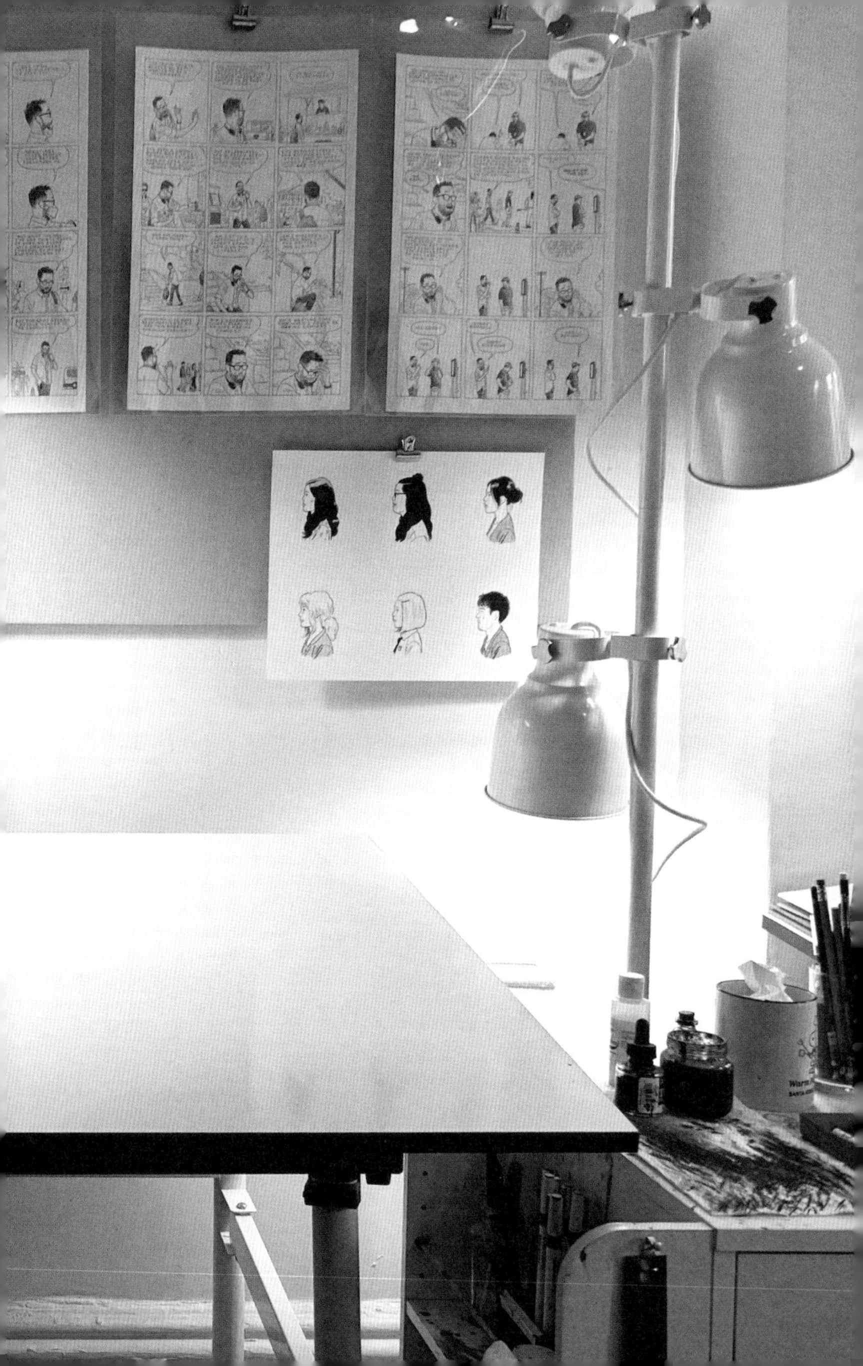

Q: *How do you scan such a large piece of work? Do you have a large-format scanner at home? (If so, which?) Or do you take it to a place to have it scanned? This has been a problem for me—it's hard to find an accessible scanner-printer with a scan area larger than A4, specialized large-format scanners are extremely expensive, and print shops usually give a terrible result on their regular Xerox copy machines.*

A: I have a very old Microtek 9800XL large-format scanner that I've had since probably 2004. It's slow and loud, but it works just well enough that I haven't been motivated to replace it. I wouldn't necessarily recommend this, but if you're trying to save money, you can download software that will allow you to use old, outdated scanners like this with modern computers.

Q: *Did you get the books I sent ya?*

A: Yes! Sorry I haven't responded directly, but they look great. And to everyone who has sent me books (or intends to do so), I apologize in advance if I'm unable to respond, give a quote, or post about them on Instagram. I try to look at everything I receive, but it's become very difficult to keep up. I hope to be a voracious reader and diligent responder in my "empty nest" and "nursing home" phases of life.

Q: *Can I adapt one of your stories into a short film? It would only be a student project, and not released commercially.*

A: All film/TV rights inquiries should be directed to Charles Ferraro and Keya Khayatian at United Talent Agency. Their contact info is on my website. But in general, I'd strongly recommend generating your own material for a student project. It's not like any of my stories are particularly "high concept," and you could probably come up with similar—if not better—ideas on your own. (Also, I hate to be so blunt, but what would I get out of this?)

Q: *How do you go about the process of finding the story you want to tell?*

A: I'd have a different answer if making comics or writing scripts was easy for me. I'd love to be the kind of prolific guy who could just bash out a bunch of things in a year, and some of them are good and some of them not so good, but who cares? But given my perfectionistic/obsessional/ avoidant work style, I need to find a story that's interesting or challenging enough to pull me through the long, slow process. Usually it's the kind of story that starts to branch off and spark other ideas, maybe even more than I can incorporate. I know I'm onto something when I basically know too much about the characters or the setting or whatever. But having all that information in reserve is inspiring and comforting, kind of like having a well-stocked kitchen even though you're making a simple soup.

In general, I try to gravitate towards stories that I think no one else would tell, at least not in the same way. Drawing from my own life experiences and allowing my own thoughts and personality to imbue the work helps make a story more specifically my own. Unfortunately, I now have to also take into account my past work and try my best to avoid repeating myself, but that's a fair trade-off for a long career.

Q: *If one of the major superhero publishers came knocking and said, "Pick a character or characters and do whatever the hell you want," what would be your answer?*

A: I actually did receive an offer similar to this many years ago. I take that back: I didn't think for a minute that it was a legitimate offer of any kind. It was more like awkward banter between two people from vastly different sectors of the comics industry who somehow found themselves seated next to each other. It was something along the lines of, "If I hypothetically gave you the opportunity, what would you do with [multi-billion dollar superhero property that I know you loved as a kid]?"

But I did give it some thought, then impulsively blurted out what I thought was genuinely a pretty good idea. To say that it was not well received would be an understatement, and I think there was a perception that I was being a wise-ass. But I wasn't, and I still think it's a pretty good idea.

I don't really get why someone would want to give away ideas or characters that they love in exchange for a work-for-hire contract. I know it's just a different mindset from the way I've worked with my publishers, but I can't help but wonder if it isn't a little heartbreaking to see your work passed on to other artists to play with, or to have it appear, uncredited, as a component of a massive Hollywood blockbuster. I think that would be too hard for me.

Q: *In "Killing and Dying" the protagonist retells a Sarah Silverman joke (among others). Could you point me to the source it's from? And while on the subject, what was the starting point of this story? This story feels very realistic.*

A: For some reason, I've had a tough time finding a clip of that Sarah Silverman joke. I know it was from some televised stand-up performance, and that I saw it on YouTube at some point years ago. I probably mangled it in my recollection, but I feel like that's appropriate given the context. Apologies to Sarah Silverman, who I imagine would be very confounded if she ever read this (or the "Killing and Dying" story).

The starting point for this story was an experience I had in the late 90s, when Dan Clowes and I stumbled upon an open mic comedy show at a café in Berkeley. It was, well...let's say "unforgettable." (Although "unbearable" and "excruciating" are also words that come to mind.) The characters and the plot all came to me many years later—mainly as a projection of my fears as a new parent—but much of the "comedy" material came directly from that night.

It would probably sound a lot cooler if I said that I had brought a notebook with me to that café, and that I had furiously sketched and transcribed the raw material for later use. But I've never been one of those guys. For the most part, I don't like to carry a sketchbook and a pen around, and I'm generally too self-conscious to draw in public. More to the point, I had no idea that what I was witnessing would inspire...anything, really. But it was one of those things that just never left my brain, and over the years Dan and I would sometimes remind each other of some of the most memorable bits from that night. Eventually I had the basic idea for the story, and then every detail from that open mic comedy show came flooding back.

Q: *Do you ever do sketches for fans?*

A: I'm terrible at off-the-cuff drawing, especially while people are watching, but I'm happy to do a little unimpressive sketch for anyone at a book signing event.*

---

* But I mean it when I say "unimpressive." I once drew a sketch for a young couple in Holland and when I was done, they silently walked away. A few seconds later, they came back and handed the book to me and asked, "Can you make it better?"

Q: *Now that you're venturing into films and noticing that you're a film fan, I have a question. In film, emotions can be conveyed via camera movements, music, sound design, etc. Unfortunately that's not the case in comics, which is more static. How do you convey characters' emotions more easily and interestingly in comics by overcoming the limitations of the medium which are not there in film?*

A: I think film and comics both have their limitations, and neither is inherently better for conveying characters' emotions. For a long time, I tried to resist a lot of the aspects of cartooning that I felt were too comic book-y, like sound effects, thought balloons, motion lines, etc., but they can be really great, useful tools, offering opportunities that film can't. And for the record, I think a static image can be incredibly powerful in terms of conveying emotion, even within a film.

Q: *What surprised you the most about the responses you received from readers about* Shortcomings*?*

A: I was very surprised and flattered that, for the first time, I had created characters that people referred to by name and felt strongly about, almost as if they were real. I think there was a vagueness or maybe a brevity to my prior stories that led people to refer to the characters more like "that guy who goes out with his ex-girlfriend" or something like that. It was definitely an adjustment for me, and there were times when *Shortcomings* first came out when someone would refer to a character by name, and I'd be like, "Who?"

In some cases, the reaction to the characters was fairly negative, and I think it was the first time I really wrestled with the idea of "likability." I've learned a lot from that experience, both in terms of craft but also in terms of separating myself from the fictional characters I create. I was initially taking all the criticism way too personally, and I had to fight the urge to respond to the numerous critical comments that emerged, particularly online.

I was also surprised by the curiosity people had about how autobiographical the story was, but I probably shouldn't have been. It was a somewhat provocative book that was filled with little details that almost dared readers to have that kind of response, and yet—I was kind of indignant! I guess I was more surprised by the comfort people felt in terms of asking me very direct, even confrontational questions. There were many times when someone would point to a panel or line of dialogue from the book and say something like, "Did you really say that?" or "Do you agree with that?" At an event at the Harvard Book Store, a guy raised his hand and said, "I had to read your book for a class, and I was wondering: is your wife white or Asian?"

As I said, it was very much a learning experience, and I'm ultimately grateful for a strong response to whatever I do. Believe me: I know firsthand that a deafening silence is way worse.

ben tanaka asshole

All   Images   Videos   News   Shopping   ⋮ More

About 3,020 results (0.22 seconds)

Blogger.com
http://warren-peace.blogspot.com › 2007/09 › optic-nerv... ⋮

Optic Nerve: Ben Tanaka needs a punch in the face

Sep 5, 2007 — Okay, that's a bit strong, but **Ben Tanaka** is a bit of an **asshole**. Adrian Tomine really crafted a reprehensible guy here; he's of Japanese ...

inkmagazinevcu.com
https://inkmagazinevcu.com › shortcomings-not-your-... ⋮

Shortcomings: Not Your Model Minority - ink magazine

Sep 17, 2023 — "Shortcomings" is a movie about an ass****. As the film opens, we're introduced to the main character, **Ben Tanaka**, doing what he does best: ...

WordPress.com
https://ditto004.wordpress.com › category › shortcomings ⋮

Shortcomings | Reading Between the Lines

Jun 4, 2013 — Adrian Tomine's Shortcomings is relentlessly negative, argumentative, and filled with "**asshole**" characters, yet it is strikingly realistic and ...

ForReel
https://thisisforreel.com › home › sundance-2023-movie-... ⋮

SUNDANCE 2023 | Movie Review: "Shortcomings"

Jan 31, 2023 — It's a story constructed around the epitome of a narcissistic **asshole** ... The role is that of one **Ben Tanaka**, a ... **Ben Tanaka** may not like this, ...

Every Movie Has a Lesson
https://everymoviehasalesson.com › blog › movie-review... ⋮

MOVIE REVIEW: Shortcomings

Aug 9, 2023 — **LESSON** #2: THE DEFINITION OF A BAD BOYFRIEND– As it turns out, **Ben** is a full-time **asshole** with an inherently bad personality. He devalues Miko ...

Q: *I was wondering about the process or ways of reaching out to your favorite cartoonists or writers. How did you do it when you were younger? Did you just send them your comics, or did you also include letters about what you loved about their work (i.e. fan mail)? What's appropriate? And is it too forward to even send your work out for critique to the artists you admire?*

A: I started sending my work (in the form of Xeroxed mini-comics) to cartoonists that I admired when I was around 16 or 17. (This was back in the pre-internet era, and most "underground" or "alternative" cartoonists published a mailing address in their comics.) I have no idea what gave me the confidence to do something like this, nor do I recall what I thought might come of it. I just remember feeling this kind of sad, desperate longing to somehow connect with, really, anyone who cared or knew about cartooning. Most of all, I think I was hungry for objective feedback and encouragement from outside of my existing audience (i.e. my mom, my dad, and my brother).

The fact that many of these cartoonists responded at all was shocking and inspiring enough, but a lot of them went above and beyond any reasonable expectations.

One person* wrote me a note asking if I was familiar with the work of Osamu Tezuka. I wrote back saying I had heard of Tezuka, but hadn't really seen much of his work. (This was long before the floodgates opened on manga translations in North America.) A week later I received a giant box filled with Japanese editions of Tezuka books, with a note saying something along the lines of, "I hope you're inspired. Return these when you're done." Several people "plugged" my amateur comics in their professional comics, imploring their readership to send money to my p.o. box. A trio of cartoonists collectively recommended my work to Chris Oliveros at Drawn & Quarterly, who soon thereafter offered to publish my work. In a few cases, an ongoing correspondence was struck up, and lifelong friendships were born.

I should also mention that there were some people who never responded at all, and a few who responded in ways that were off-putting or unkind. But honestly, any response at all from the world beyond my bedroom—especially from people that I thought of the way normal people think of sports heroes—was unbelievable and invigorating.

_____

* As much as I'd like to identify and thank these people by name, I'm going to preserve their anonymity, both for the sake of their privacy and so that they're not suddenly inundated by requests from people expecting the same response.

Obviously I can't guarantee that everyone will have similar experiences, but to answer your question: I don't think there's anything inappropriate about sending your work to artists you admire. It probably is inappropriate to expect a certain kind of response, or even any response at all. And it definitely wouldn't hurt to include a brief note, including at least a tiny bit of praise for the recipient's work.* Also, if you specifically ask for feedback, be prepared to take some criticism or advice that you maybe weren't expecting.

---

* This may sound like common sense, but you'd be surprised.

Q: *I hope you were able to get my letter in the mail back in 2017 when I asked for a podcast interview. LOL.*

A: Apologies if you really did send that letter and I didn't respond. I'm sure it's moot now, but for anyone reading this, please direct these kinds of inquiries to Drawn & Quarterly's director of marketing, Julia Pohl-Miranda. Her email address is: julia@drawnandquarterly.com, and she's much more organized and responsible about this stuff than I am.

Q: *Do you have any how-to books for writing/cartooning/ etc. that you've found especially helpful or significant?*

A: I think the best how-to books about cartooning are just the books that contain the best cartooning. I learned the most about making comics from studying, copying, and then trying to learn how to not copy from the work of my favorite cartoonists. There's something magical about really dissecting a comic you love, trying to figure out how and why it affects you so much, and then trying to replicate that. But for whatever reason, the two instructional books from my childhood that remain clearest in my memory (and that I still have on my bookshelf) are *How to Draw Comics the Marvel Way* by Stan Lee and John Buscema and *Drawing the Head & Figure* by Jack Hamm.

And before everyone starts composing outraged messages like "But what about such-and-such book?," I want to clarify that there simply weren't very many "how-to" books available during my formative years. I know many people who have benefited immensely from the numerous books that have been published in more modern times, including those by Lynda Barry, Ivan Brunetti, and Scott McCloud.

Q: I just wanted to ask what your favorite single floppy comic is? My favorite is either Acme Novelty Library *#1,* Optic Nerve *#1, or* Eightball *#16.*

A: Ooh, this is a tough one. Since you picked three, I'll do the same. (And just to clarify, by "favorite" I mean "most historically/personally significant in terms of my artistic development.")

Amazing Spider-Man #151

This was my first "favorite" comic. I honestly can't remember anything about the story itself, but the John Romita cover is burned into my memory, and I know I was inspired to make many primitive attempts at replicating it with pencils and crayons. Since it was published only a year after my birth, I'm assuming it was one of the countless comics that my brother Dylan bought and passed on to me. I know that at some point, it became so worn that my mom affixed a piece of masking tape along the spine to hold the cover in place, and the pristine, tape-less versions I'm currently looking at online seem glaringly incomplete.

Love and Rockets #20

You know how musicians talk about the album that changed their life? This was my version of that. I was thirteen years old, and I was (probably belatedly) growing disenchanted with the superhero comics I'd been collecting my whole life. I bought this issue on a whim, and it instantly became clear to me that I had lost interest in the subject matter of superhero comics, not the medium itself. It sounds so obvious to say that now, but it was a different world in 1987 (especially in Fresno, California). I was immediately, profoundly changed by the work of both Jaime and Gilbert Hernandez, and I literally said to myself, "This is what I want to do."

Eightball #12

In 1993, a UC Berkeley classmate of mine named Erika introduced me to her fiancé, who just happened to be one of the greatest cartoonists to ever live. Yes, this is the seemingly impossible way that I met Daniel Clowes. Even more preposterous was the fact that we lived on the same street, less than a block away from each other. Erika and Dan soon became my favorite people in Berkeley, and I had the privilege of seeing issue 12 of *Eightball* reveal itself page by page in Dan's studio when I visited their apartment. I can't overstate the impact of not only seeing those incredible pages in person and in progress, but also just seeing what a cartoonist's life could look like. So, obviously I have a very specific, personal connection to this particular comic, but it's also just one of the best comics I've ever read.

Q: *Hi! As an aspiring comic artist, I wonder how you deal with the vulnerability you show in your comics? It has always made me nervous and self-conscious to portrait parts of myself in comics. How do you make yourself feel okay about people knowing who you are and what you think? For instance,* The Loneliness of the Long-Distance Cartoonist *is really personal, what helps you to be brave enough to share such personal and vulnerable stories?*

A: I understand that feeling of self-consciousness all too well, and I think the only reason I'm able to publish the work I do is that I started on this path before I knew any better. My earliest published comics were just excerpts from private sketchbooks—things that I scribbled out strictly for my own practice or amusement. And when I started to slowly share that work with friends and family, it was clear that it was that personal, private quality that people responded to more than anything else. (It certainly wasn't my drawing ability!) So that encouraged me to keep working in that same direction. I probably would've ended up on a different path if my earliest readers had said, "Ugh, this is too vulnerable!"

Over the course of my career, I felt that sense of self-consciousness return in waves, especially once my work started to get more widely distributed and reviewed. In some ways, getting good reviews made it worse because then there was a "devil's advocate" response of "Well, he's not *that* good." And I talked about this earlier, but as I pushed myself to write more ambitious stories, there was an uptick in interest in terms of what was autobiographical and what was fiction.

Basically, it's an ongoing struggle! I've found it helpful to try to trick myself back into that earliest creative mindset, where I'm just creating the work for its own sake. I really recommend the idea of creating work but telling yourself it's not for publication (and then putting it out there if it happens to turn out well). As a reader, I very much value work that is personal, vulnerable, even exposing, but I know that's not comfortable or even possible for some people. In which case, don't torture yourself.

Q: *I'm so glad you opened up these questions, I have one in particular that's been burning in my mind for the past few years since I read* The Loneliness of the Long-Distance Cartoonist. *I researched online but couldn't seem to find you mentioning the answer in any interviews about the book. I must (simply must!) know who the venerable cartoonist was that you interacted with at a party who mentioned that he "loves jujitsu" on page 90 of your book. Thanks and hopefully you are allowed to answer this!*

A: Well, he's dead now, so I almost feel comfortable telling you, but...no. It still doesn't feel right. Sorry. And just for the record: he was old, it didn't feel malicious, and it didn't affect my admiration of his work. (Also, if you read the scene carefully, I never say outright that he was a cartoonist!)

The Loneliness of the Long-Distance Cartoonist (2020)

Q: *Your stories appear to be so personal. I was wondering if anyone has ever had an issue with how they were portrayed?*

A: I'm tempted to whitewash this in an effort to encourage more people to create personal work, but the short, honest answer is: yes.

Q: *Adrian, we have kids that go to school in the same neighborhood. I'd love to hear your take on encouraging children to read and write comics and the general value of comics for young readers.*

A: I don't have any kind of prescriptive or philosophical answer here, but I did encourage both of my kids to read and create comics. They will humbly disagree with me, but I think the comics they've created over the years are incredible, and I'm astounded by how much of the story-telling is intuitive and free of outside influence. My experience is that if you create a page of blank panels and give that to a kid, they will immediately start creating a comic. And you will be surprised and delighted by what they create.

In terms of reading, comics have played a big part in both of my kids' process of learning to read. Raina Telgemeier's autobiographical graphic novels were the first books that my older daughter got completely absorbed in. She read each of them in a single sitting, and then promptly began rereading them. She's in high school now, but I have a hunch she'll still be first in line for Raina's next book. My younger daughter has dyslexia, and the *Peanuts* collections have provided a major step towards her reading and enjoying books on her own. It's very moving for me to see her struggle through the first three panels of a strip and then actually laugh out loud upon reading the fourth.

It might seem like all of this could be attributed to my own personal interests or a general pro-comics bias in our household, but I've seen and heard similar stories from almost all of our family friends. It's genuinely a different world than the one we grew up in, and it seems like the appeal of comics is just common knowledge to all kids—and more significantly, totally free of any stigma. And in case anyone has concerns about the long-term impact of reading comics on young kids, I'm happy to report that my older daughter and all her friends have grown up to be excellent students, good humans, and readers of all different sorts of books.

Q: *Do you ever ask for your colleagues' opinions during the creation process, or do you only share the manuscript with them once the work is finished?*

A: From 1993 to 2003, I lived in close proximity to my two closest cartoonist friends, Richard Sala and Daniel Clowes. We didn't explicitly solicit feedback from each other, but we saw each other a lot, and it was only natural that we would talk about whatever we were working on at the time. We'd also go to each other's homes and see (and talk about) whatever artwork was currently in progress.* That was the closest I ever had to a gang of colleagues, and especially as the rookie of the group, it was profoundly inspiring and educational.

Nowadays, my main source of feedback is my wife, and sometimes my kids. Dan is still my closest artist friend, but we live on opposite coasts. I'll occasionally solicit his advice, especially in recent years with regards to various film projects, but it's mostly done via text or email. Here in New York I have a group of very smart, literary friends—writers, editors, critics—and their casual influence and feedback has been invaluable. My editor at

* Actually, we never spent time at Richard's home, but that's another story.

Drawn & Quarterly, Tracy Hurren, has improved my recent books (including this one) in countless ways, above and beyond what her job title might imply.

But for the most part, I do the work on my own, hope for the best, and hear what people think once it's finished.

Q: *Have you ever been tempted to create a much more extensive work that covers your entire life?*

A: I do have an outline and notes for another autobiographical book—one which would be less specifically focused on my relationship with comics—but it would still make some pretty significant time leaps. I don't think anyone (including myself) is interested in a comprehensive life story!

Q: *Were you ever scared that making art as your job might make you hate making art?*

A: I don't think I was ever scared of that in an anticipatory way because I had no idea that it was a possibility. But unfortunately there have been times where it has, in fact, happened. Reaching a wider audience and opening myself up to greater levels of criticism was definitely hard. In the earlier years of my career, I did a lot more illustration work to support myself, and some of those jobs—particularly ones in the advertising/merchandising sector—made me hate everything, not just the act of making art. And probably the most challenging period was when my wife was in grad school, we had two young kids, and I was trying to support all of us. The idea that my next paycheck would arrive when I turned in a graphic novel that ultimately took seven years to complete put me in a headspace that, ironically, made completing that graphic novel pretty tough. At each of those points in my life, I often fantasized about having a quiet office, a steady paycheck, and an employee benefits package. The fact that I've (so far) always found my way back to loving my job tells me that it's probably the thing I'm best suited to.

Q: *I find that your work has such a specific sense of place. How does that play into your creative process? Are you coming up with characters first and then settings, or do you sometimes start with a location or setting?*

A: That's a great compliment because the specific details of location and setting have always been very important to me, but I feel like it's the kind of thing that's invisible to the casual reader. All of my *New Yorker* covers have involved a fair amount of research and life drawing, even if it's just for something as insignificant as what the seats on the subway look like. Before it was an actual movie, *Shortcomings* (the graphic novel) was created almost like a movie on paper. I did a lot of "pre-production" work that included figuring out real world locations for every scene, and then trying to depict those locations as accurately as possible.

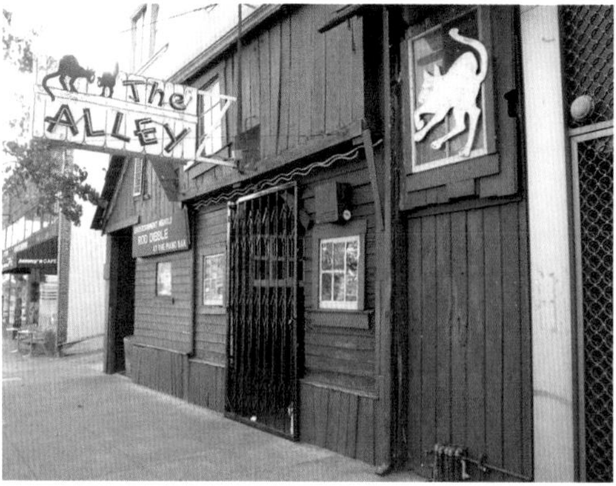
The
ALLEY

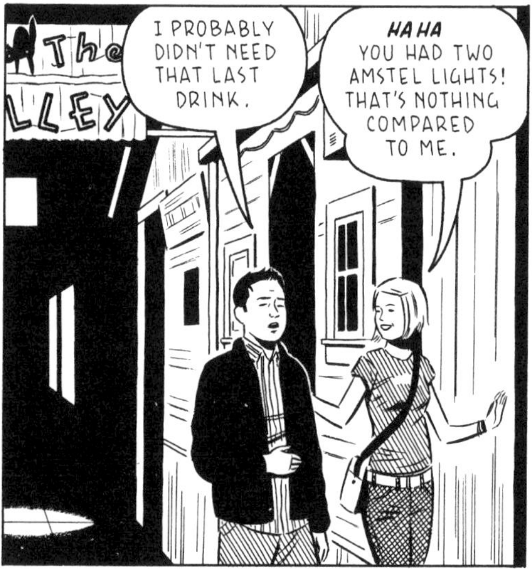
The
LLEY
I PROBABLY DIDN'T NEED THAT LAST DRINK.
HA HA YOU HAD TWO AMSTEL LIGHTS! THAT'S NOTHING COMPARED TO ME.

Shortcomings (2007)

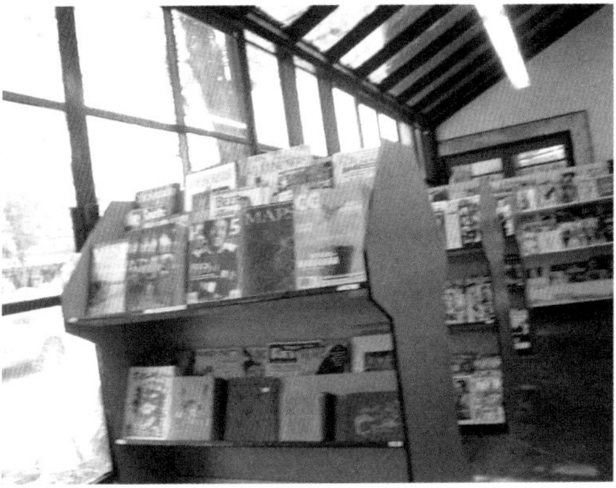

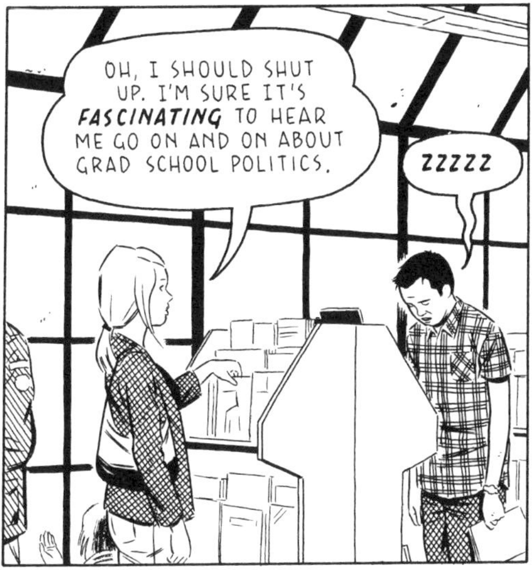
OH, I SHOULD SHUT UP. I'M SURE IT'S *FASCINATING* TO HEAR ME GO ON AND ON ABOUT GRAD SCHOOL POLITICS.
ZZZZZ

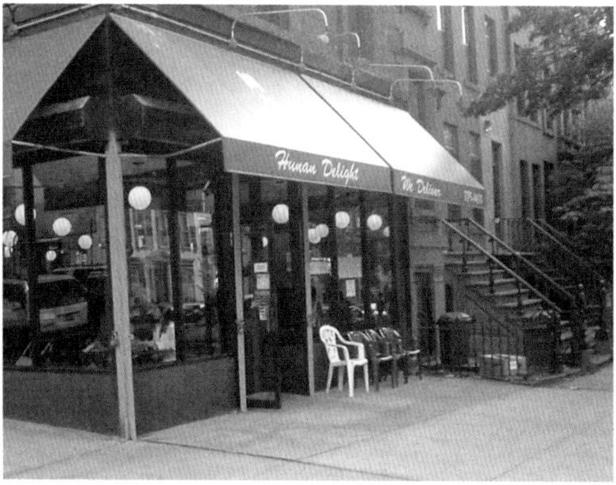
Hunan Delight
We Deliver

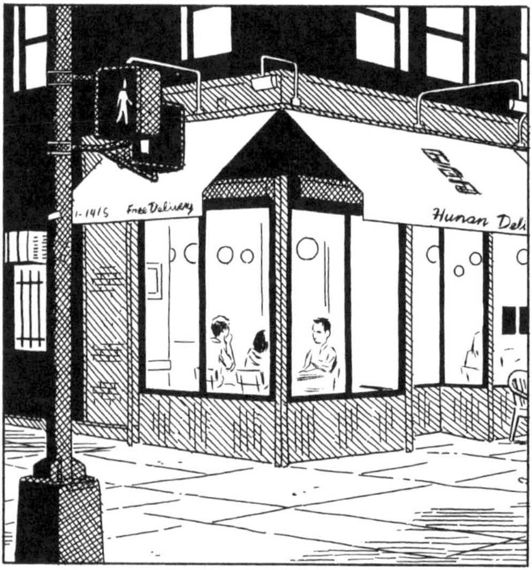
1-1415 Free Delivery
Hunan Deli

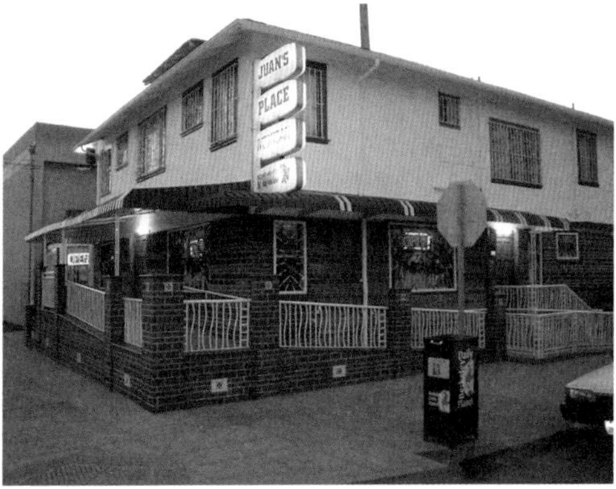
JUAN'S
PLACE

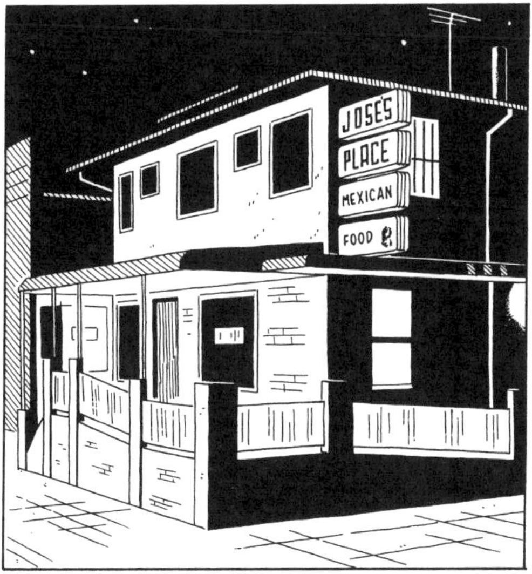
JOSE'S
PLACE
MEXICAN
FOOD

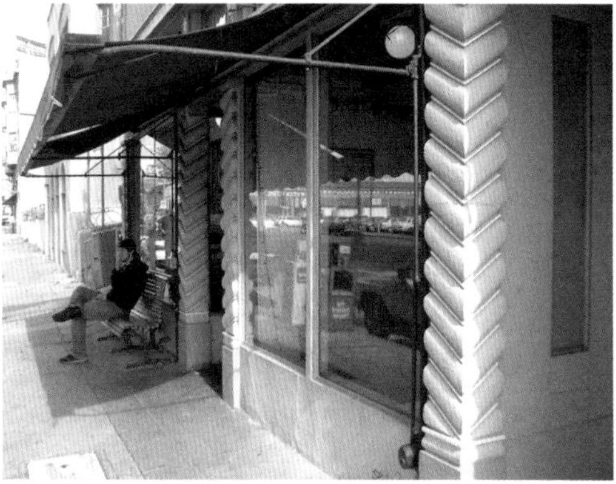

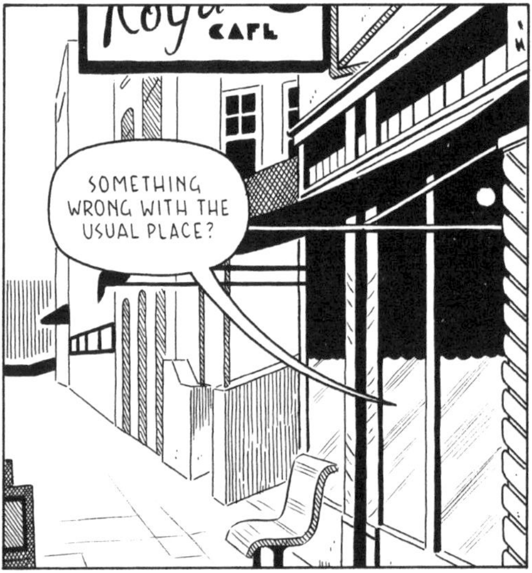
CAFE
SOMETHING WRONG WITH THE USUAL PLACE?

Even shorter stories of mine take place in very specific locations, although it's never made explicit. For example, "Bomb Scare" is set in the suburbs of Sacramento. "Intruders" mostly takes place in the apartment that I lived in on College Avenue in Berkeley. The cover of *Killing and Dying* is an amalgamation of intersections in Oakland, Emeryville, and Pasadena.

I have no idea if these decisions have any impact on the experience of reading the stories, but they feel to me like a crucial part of the creative process. Somehow, just deciding on a setting—particularly one that I can conjure from memory—instantly unlocks all kinds of ideas that wouldn't have come to me otherwise. My hope is that this might enrich the stories on a subliminal level, and if nothing else, it's an endeavor that I find oddly satisfying.

Q: *You've drawn several* New Yorker *covers about books and bookstores. Do you have any thoughts or memories or anecdotes about bookstores?*

A: I never went to art school, and I never received any kind of formal training about how to make comics or how to be a cartoonist. Instead, I had countless afternoons spent with two seasoned veterans: the aforementioned Richard Sala and Daniel Clowes. A lot of those afternoons were spent in diners and cafés, but I learned the most on our regular trips to various Bay Area comic shops and bookstores. Richard and Dan were always very humble and generous, and they treated me like a peer when they had no good reason to. I played along and tried to act like I was familiar with all the various books they picked up and discussed and sometimes fought over, but I was actually getting an education. I was taking mental notes, absorbing their every word, and casually learning about a seemingly endless pantheon of writers, artists, and cartoonists from the past. In a pre-internet world, there really was no other way I would've learned about someone like Alex Toth or Helen E. Hokinson or Crockett Johnson. So: eternal gratitude to Dan and Richard, and also to Comic Relief, Dr. Comics and Mr. Games, Pegasus Books, Cody's, Kayo, Moe's, Serendipity, etc. etc.

Q: *Being an artist takes a lot from you, but (I think/hope) it's given a lot in return. Would you say it's given more than it's taken?*

A: This is an easy one. I actually don't think that being an artist has taken that much from me, and in fact, almost everything that I love about my present life can be traced back to the decision I made to start putting my teenage scribbles out into the world.

Q: *Do you have any general advice for aspiring illustrators/graphic novelists/screenwriters?*

A: This is probably the hardest question for me to answer both because it's so broad, and because I often still feel like an aspiring illustrator/graphic novelist/screenwriter myself. I've managed to make a job out of it, but in each of those fields I've fallen far short of my aspirations and am always struggling to get even a little bit closer. So I'm really still trying to figure it all out myself. But let me try to share a few thoughts, if not hard advice.

A few years ago I gave a talk at an art school in Manhattan, and I could tell that the students were quickly losing interest in my admittedly ponderous presentation. So in an attempt to regain their attention, I asked the students what their goals were. A guy in the back of the room quickly blurted out, "To do whatever the fuck I want and get rich doing it!" Some of the other students cringed and recoiled, but just as many shook their heads in tacit agreement. I was instantly overcome by feelings of rage and contempt—but also irrelevance, like there was nothing I could really say that would help that guy achieve his goals. I tried to respond in a tactful manner, but I'm sure there was more than a hint of passive aggression in my words.

I'll admit: my immediate thought was, "God, what an obnoxious, entitled creep!" But when I heard some of the other students' answers, I found that many of them were vague, muddled, or conflicted. I struggled (and failed miserably) to give advice to a guy who said only that he wanted to "effect change." I still thought the first person was an obnoxious, entitled creep, but at least he had a clear goal.

And then, as I stood on the subway platform headed home, I felt an all-too-familiar type of cringe washing over me. I hadn't exactly spent my life hiding my drawings in the floorboards of my house, and I certainly hadn't refused financial compensation for my work. In fact, that obnoxious creep had actually articulated *my* life goals, distilled to their most crass, naked form. I literally gasped as the depth of my hypocrisy revealed itself. As is often the case for me after leaving various meetings or events in Manhattan, I had a momentary urge to leap into the subway tracks as the next train approached.

All of which is to say I think it's important for aspiring artists to be honest with themselves and really think about what they're aiming for. In hindsight I can see that I took a very scattershot approach to my work, often wasting time pursuing something I didn't want or ignoring the thing I did. If someone wants to simply be an artist, to express themself, to create work that they love, then really the only way they could possibly fail is by not sitting down and doing the work. If someone wants to make a career of it, that's another story. And if they, in all honesty, just want to get rich and famous, that's something else entirely. I can't give concrete advice for all of those different possible paths, other than to say it helps a lot to know which path you're on.

When I was thinking about how to best answer this question, I kept coming up with specific, prescriptive bits of advice that would basically guide someone towards making the kind of work that I would like. And I realized that's not really helpful, especially for someone who might have totally different tastes and interests. But one suggestion that I thought might be applicable to all (or most) aspiring cartoonists or screenwriters is the idea of writing or creating from a place that's specific to you. I don't mean everything has to be autobiographical or even semi-autobiographical. I just mean allowing some of your own authentic feelings, opinions, idiosyncrasies, and experiences to inform the work, regardless of how you think that might be received. Even if that personal angle is deeply sublimated in a completely made-up genre

story or spread out across a cast of fully fictional characters, I think it will enhance the work in all kinds of ways,
both for you and the audience. This seems like a pretty
obvious bit of advice, but maybe it's a tiny counterbal-
ance to the overwhelming emphasis these days on con-
cepts, plots, spectacle, and "intellectual property."

The other suggestion that comes to mind isn't necessarily something that will improve your art (although
it might), but it's more like something cool that you can
do because you're an artist. And that is: make something
while you think about someone you love who's died. I
know it sounds macabre, but stick with me. A few years
ago, I drew an illustration based on a photo of my grand-
mother when she was a young woman. I spent over a
week working on it, and during that time I recalled more
memories and felt more connected to her than I had in
many years. I was thinking about how to draw her, but I
also found myself thinking about her life and our time together. I had a similar experience recently with a play I've
been working on. I was struggling with a certain line, and
somehow I had the idea to quote an inadvertently funny
thing my dad once said. I thought it would be a little "in
joke" that maybe my wife or my brother might chuckle at.
But as soon as I typed it out, I could hear my dad saying it

"San Francisco, 1942," after Dorothea Lange (2021)

as if he was there in the room, and the fictional character I'd given the line to immediately felt more idiosyncratic, nuanced, and alive. At a table read of the script, I had the surreal experience of seeing a great actor utter that silly line of my dad's. It got an unexpectedly big laugh right where I needed it, and it sent a shiver down my spine, nearly bringing me to tears. It was several years since my dad's death, and it felt like he had given me something. I know that many people regularly experience these kinds of vaguely cosmic, time-traveling mental connections at funerals, cemeteries, and places of worship, but for me it happens most deeply within the process of writing or drawing. I can't promise the same results for you, but I still recommend trying it.

Finally, this is probably the most nebulous part of my already rambling answer, but maybe it will be useful to someone, especially parents of aspiring artists. I had what might be described as an unsettled childhood, one that was deeply affected by things like my parents' divorce, a lot of moving around, and a socially awkward, obsessive personality. Obviously I wouldn't recommend any of these things if they can be avoided, but I'm also absolutely certain that my career exists as a direct result of them. I basically taught myself to write and draw as a protective defense against chaos and loneliness. On the other hand, for five years during my childhood I had the privilege of taking weekly piano lessons from a talented, strict, and patient teacher. I never missed a lesson, I diligently practiced for the mandated thirty minutes per day, and I never developed anything close to proficiency. I quickly lost all interest in piano and couldn't play a simple tune now to save my life. Make of this what you will, but just from personal experience I've noticed that there are long-term effects to everything, and they're often paradoxical.

Q: *What are you working on now? What's next?*

A: I'm working on a bunch of different things, all in various stages of evolution: a play, a couple books, a few screenplays. A lot of it will probably never come to fruition, but regardless, I'm really enjoying the work. It's a great feeling to be equally excited about a variety of projects, and to be able to bounce from one to the other.

As I type this, though, one of my kids has a bad ear infection and the other one, due to various holidays and closures, only has nine full days of school this month. So right now—and at this point in my life in general—I'm trying to accept and enjoy the fact that I'm not as productive an artist as I have been in the past. It was something I resisted for a long time, but the truth is I currently feel more like a dad than anything else. I know that will sound extremely depressing to many young, unencumbered artists, but as someone who has spent much of his life lonely, self-involved, and work-obsessed, I consider it a kind of success.

Q: *So now that you've done this book, is that it? Are you cutting us off?*

A: I'm afraid so. I think we can all agree that I've said more than enough, and that now is as good a time as any to end this slightly awkward, obligatory interaction. Thanks and farewell.

Just kidding! I may not always be able to respond directly, but I will continue to read every single card, letter, and message for as long as I'm physically and mentally able. Even beyond that, probably.

Adrian Tomine was born in 1974 in Sacramento, California. His other books include *The Loneliness of the Long-Distance Cartoonist*, *Killing and Dying*, *Summer Blonde*, and *Sleepwalk and Other Stories*. He wrote the screenplay for the feature film adaptation of *Shortcomings*, and stories from *Killing and Dying* and *Summer Blonde* were adapted into the film *Paris, 13th District*. Since 1999, his illustrations have appeared regularly on the cover and in the pages of *The New Yorker*. He lives in Brooklyn, New York with his wife and daughters.